LEGENDS
AND LORE
OF
BIRMINGHAM
& CENTRAL ALABAMA

LEGENDS
AND LORE
OF
BIRMINGHAM
& CENTRAL ALABAMA

BEVERLY CRIDER

THE
History
PRESS

Published by The History Press
Charleston, SC 29403
www.historypress.net

Copyright © 2014 by Beverly Crider
All rights reserved

Unless otherwise noted, images come from the public domain.

First published 2014

Manufactured in the United States

ISBN 978.1.62619.396.3

Library of Congress CIP data applied for.

CONTENTS

CONTENTS

CONTENTS

INTRODUCTION

Southerners are generally known for the ability to spin a good yarn. I'm certainly known for my gift of gab, but that "yarn-spinning" thing…well, let's just say I'm no Kathryn Tucker Windham. That's for sure! As Twitter, Facebook, Instagram and other real-time forms of communication have taken control of our lives, forcing us to condense, abbreviate and otherwise cut our messages down to the bare bones, I'm afraid that the ability to tell a good tale may eventually become even harder to find than it is today.

I remember my early attempts at writing when I was in elementary school. I let my imagination run wild, and my schoolteachers encouraged me. I remember standing in front of my classmates reading my latest attempt at a short story, and I just knew that one day I would write an exciting full-length novel. As I began journalism classes in college, I had to stop myself from using too many adjectives or going into too much detail when writing a news story. Even way back then, before the fast-paced Internet newsfeeds, we were already becoming impatient readers. It was really difficult in the beginning. Then, somewhere along the way, I discovered that the short-handed approach had become the way I wrote everything. I found myself constantly editing the words on the page, making the final product shorter and shorter to fit the requirements of the media. When I attempted to write more "creative" pieces, I found myself questioning the need for "all those words." (Which is a laugh, because I have no such qualms about using words in conversation, as anyone who knows me can confirm.)

As we lose our storytellers, we lose our stories. That might sound pretty obvious, but think about it. Gone are the days of sitting on the porch, "shooting the breeze." Our stories are becoming more homogenous as a nation. That's not necessarily a bad thing, but it would be nice to keep some of those regional stories alive. So, let me cut to the chase and move things along. While this is not a detailed, comprehensive volume about Central Alabama's people, places and things, I hope you will find it somehow bridges the gap between today's status updates and yesterday's handwritten letters.

PART I

LEGENDARY RESIDENTS

CHAPTER 1

MUMMY DEAREST

S trapped to the sideboard of a Ford Model-T, Hazel the Mummy bounced down the roads of Alabama and beyond, bringing a hefty income of $150–$200 per week for her owner, Orlando Clayton Brooks, during the early part of the twentieth century. How, exactly, Hazel became a mummy is the stuff legends are made of.

Hazel Farris was born sometime around 1880 in Kentucky. As a young newlywed, some twenty years later, Harris had developed quite the knack for spending money. Some say she was particularly fond of hats. Apparently, she purchased (or expressed interest in purchasing) one hat too many, over which her husband became outraged. On the morning of April 6, 1905, during a struggle that ensued over the hat purchase, Hazel shot and killed her husband. Three policemen happened to be walking by and heard the shots. When they arrived at the home, they found Hazel standing over her husband's body holding a gun. She shot the three officers as well.

By now, quite a crowd had gathered. The deputy sheriff tried to take her in to custody but succeeded only in shooting off the ring finger of one of her hands before she returned a deadly shot. She fled her pursuers and made her way to Bessemer, Alabama, where she took up new residence. There is some question as to how she portrayed herself to the public in her new home, although consensus seems to be that she worked as a prostitute and was known to drink heavily.

Hazel must have felt alone in this new town and developed the need to share the details of her past with someone. Unfortunately for her, she chose her new beaux, who apparently was a policeman. Law won out over love, and he turned her in. Rather than go to jail, she decided to kill herself. On December 20, 1906, she drank a fatal combination of alcohol and what many have concluded was arsenic.

Hazel's body was taken to a nearby furniture store, which served as a makeshift funeral parlor, as many furniture stores did during that time. No one claimed her body, and as it lay in the back of the store, it began to decay (or not decay) in a most unusual way. The skin became dried and tightly drawn over her skeletal remains. Some claimed her hair and nails continued to grow, although today we realize it is actually the skin receding, making the hair and nails appear to be longer.

The store owner saw the opportunity to cash in on the notoriety of the case and offered anyone interested the chance to see Hazel, propped up against a wall in the back of the store, for a mere ten cents. He then sent the mummy by train to his brother in Tuscaloosa so he could display her in the same manner.

Captain Harvey Lee Boswell (not to be confused with Lee Harvey Oswald) also exhibited Hazel's remains before traveling showman O.C. Brooks purchased the body for twenty-five dollars in May 1907.

With ticket sales bringing Brooks such a nice income, Hazel's ride was upgraded to a 1931 Oldsmobile. Brooks continued to show the mummy for another forty years. His printed handbills claimed the body was "exhibited for the benefit of science."

What mummy is not going to develop certain rumored "powers"? Hazel's power, it seemed, was to bring good luck to those who rubbed her hand. When this special ability became "known," Brooks offered Hazel's visitors the opportunity to do just that for an additional twenty-five cents. Hazel's fame continued to spread, and she reportedly appeared before royal audiences in Europe after World War II.

As the popularity of traveling circuses began to dwindle, Brooks retired to Coushatta, Louisiana, where he died on April 1, 1950. Hazel was passed down to Brooks's twelve-year-old nephew, Luther. Rumor has it that a note was found in Hazel's casket that instructed Luther never to sell her or show her as a freak…and never to bury her. If he was to show her, Luther was instructed to donate all proceeds to charity. Luther disputed any restrictions.

Luther kept Hazel in his garage in Nashville, Tennessee, and reportedly relished the fact that he was the only kid in school who owned a mummy. He showed Hazel at school carnivals, and after graduating from high school in 1958, he added carnival rides to his show. He sold the rides in 1965 but kept

---

1958 — NOW BOOKING FOR SEASON — 1958

HAZEL FARRIS

The Only Exhibit of This Type On Exhibition

Nation-Wide Tour Today!

————★————

"HAZEL FARRIS" KILLED FIVE MEN; ESCAPED TO BESSEMER, ALA., LOVED AGAIN; WAS BETRAYED TO THE OFFICERS, THEN ENDED HER OWN LIFE RATHER THAN SUBMIT TO ARREST — A GENUINE HUMAN BODY.

"Hazel" affords you a study worth while. It is the only genuine human mummy in the world today except a few "Egyptian" subjects in some of the museums in the large cities. "Hazel" is exhibited in the open air so that all may feel and examine the beautiful suit of long, flowing hair.

$500.00 FORFEIT—"Hazel" is not "petrified" nor "made to order", and the exhibitors will pay $500.00 in cash to anyone who will examine the body of "Hazel, the Mummy" and prove that it is not genuine. This is a bona fide business proposition, made in good faith and without reserve whatsoever. ANY and ALL DOCTORS specially invited to make examinations at ANY time which suits their convenience. "Hazel" is exhibited for the benefit of science.

If you are interested in booking this attraction in your city or any other type of project, write for details.

CHARLIE CAMPBELL, Exhibitor

Permanent Address

P. O. BOX 301   SYLVA, N. C.

Booking notice for the showing of Hazel Farris, the mummy.

Hazel for continued showings at schools and churches. While in Luther's care, the mummy suffered some further bodily injuries, including a broken nose.

Eventually, Luther's two daughters took over the exhibits for a short time before the Brooks family stopped promoting her and let her rest. In 1974, researchers with the Bessemer Hall of History tracked down Hazel's remains, which had become one of Bessemer's most famous legends. The Brooks family agreed to bring Hazel to Bessemer for a special exhibition in a vacant downtown building that October. Thousands of people paid fifty cents each to walk past her casket.

Hazel was returned to Bessemer on several more occasions after the city museum opened in the basement of the Bessemer Public Library. She also was brought to the Alabama State Fair and to the University of Alabama's Ferguson Center in 1975. Her final appearances in Bessemer occurred in October 1994 and 1995.

In later years, the corpse passed to the next generation of Brookses, who were not as excited about sharing their home with a mummy. They also did not feel bound by their family's early wishes. In 2002, Hazel was taken to the Pettus, Owen and Wood Funeral Home for cremation. Before the destruction of the mummy, she appeared on an episode of the National Geographic Channel's *The Mummy Road Show*.

X-ray, computed tomography (CT) and endoscopic examinations performed for the show indicated that the body was infused with high levels of arsenic, which contributed to its preservation. Arsenic was a fairly common method of embalming in the day, so there was no conclusive indication that the arsenic was taken by Hazel in a suicide attempt rather than used as part of her embalming. Blood clots were also found in her pulmonary system, but it could not be determined conclusively whether they were formed as a result of illness, such as pneumonia, or during the embalming process.

Apparently, Hazel also practiced atrocious dental hygiene, as tests showed cavities and damaged teeth. She lost her gold teeth in 1959 "when the tent fell on a Nashville carnival and a group of women accidentally turned her casket over and dumped Hazel into the sawdust," according to Luther Brooks's account in *Myths, Mysteries and Legends of Alabama*.

After National Geographic's televised autopsy, Hazel's remains were finally cremated and entombed in Madison, Tennessee.

CHAPTER 2

MYRTLE CORBIN,
THE FOUR-LEGGED WOMAN

Josephine Myrtle Corbin, a star in the sideshow or so-called freak show circuit of the late nineteenth and early twentieth centuries, was a dipygus, a rare form of conjoined twin. She had two complete bodies from the waist down: two pelvises and two separate excretory and reproductive systems. She had two small inner legs and a pair of normal-sized outer legs. Her smaller legs, which had feet with only three toes each, could move but were unable to assist with walking. Her right outer foot was clubbed, leaving Myrtle with, essentially, only one fully functioning leg.

Born on May 12, 1868, in Lincoln County, Tennessee, Myrtle was an immediate sensation in the local papers, and her case was written up in medical journals of the time.

Her father, William Corbin, was an injured Confederate veteran with little income. To put food on the table, he began showing his five-week-old daughter to visitors for a small fee. In 1870, the family moved to Blount County, Alabama, where they had another daughter, Willie Ann. Myrtle's younger sister was born "normal."

With Blount County as their base of operations, Myrtle's father began to take her around the country, exhibiting her at fairs, sideshows and "dime museums." Her first promotional material described her as being as "gentle of disposition as the summer sunshine and as happy as the day is long." At the age of fourteen, she began appearing with P.T. Barnum's traveling exhibitions, receiving an extraordinary salary of $250 per week. She became one of Barnum's most popular acts.

Myrtle Corbin, the four-legged woman.

Back at home, Willie Ann married Hiram Locke Bicknell, and Hiram's younger brother, James, who was studying to become a doctor, became attracted to Myrtle. As a well-paid performer, Myrtle was accustomed to proclamations of affection as a means of gaining access to her money. James, who would soon have a doctor's income, was different. She felt his interest was genuine. The two were married in Blount County on June 12, 1886. Myrtle retired from show business to start a family.

Myrtle's rise to fame came at a time when the medical world was fascinated with the study of physical abnormalities, or teratology. Articles about her condition and her first pregnancy appeared in such medical journals as the *Journal of the American Medical Association*, the *British Medical Journal* and the *American Journal of Obstetrics*, which described her as belonging to a class of "monsters by fusion."

Myrtle had four daughters and a son, and rumor has it that three of her children were born from one twin and two from the other. We may never know if that is true or not, but it was medically possible. The reproductive systems of both Myrtle and her twin were functional.

The Bicknells moved from their Blount County home to live a quiet life in Cleburne City, Texas, until their children moved out on their own. Myrtle returned to her show business life in 1909 at the age of forty-one.

After more than twenty years out of the limelight, she still had a knack for showmanship. As a child, she would often dress her small limbs with socks and shoes that matched her larger outer limbs. She continued do so as an adult. She appeared at Huber's Museum in New York, performed with the

Ringling Brothers Circus and appeared at Coney Island. Her performances earned her an amazing paycheck of $450 a week.

Myrtle continued her appearances for a few more years before retiring for good. In 1928, she developed a skin infection on her right leg, which was diagnosed by a Cleburne City doctor as a streptococcal infection. She died shortly thereafter on May 6, 1928.

CHAPTER 3

THE PIONEER "MADAM" WHO HELPED SAVE BIRMINGHAM

I t's a safe bet many of you have never heard of one particular Birmingham pioneer credited by many with helping the city survive its infancy. It's doubtful she's mentioned in high school history classes, even though she rests alongside Birmingham's founding fathers in Oak Hill Cemetery. That might have something to do with her occupation. She was one of the city's most successful "ladies of the evening."

It's hard to tell just where fact and fiction diverge when discussing Lou Wooster. It seems safe to assume she was born in Tuscaloosa in 1842 and moved with her family to Mobile early in life. After her father died in 1851, Lou's mother, Mary, remarried. Her new stepfather left the family soon after and took all their money with him. Mary died in 1857, leaving Lou and her sisters destitute. When Lou was fifteen, her older sister, Margaret, turned to prostitution to bring in money. Her two younger sisters were placed in Mobile's Protestant Orphan Asylum, and Lou moved to New Orleans to live with her married sister.

She returned to Mobile with a forged letter allowing her to remove her sisters from the orphanage. The girls went to live with a male family friend, and Lou later joined a Montgomery brothel. She had moved to Birmingham by at least 1873, as she was in the city during that year's deadly cholera epidemic. While thousands of people were fleeing the city, Lou, by then well known among the city's prostitutes, stayed to nurse the sick and prepare bodies for burial. She and other "working girls" converted brothels into clinics. With medical facilities overflowing with patients, Lou's clinics likely saved many lives that otherwise would have been lost.

After the epidemic, Lou had few clients left in Birmingham, so she moved to Montgomery, where she opened a brothel. A few years later, she was back in Birmingham, operating multiple brothels near city hall, where she would be closer to potential clients with hefty bank accounts.

Whether by deliberate strategy or not, the move paid off, and Lou became a wealthy Birmingham madam who donated large amounts to charity. In the 1880s, she bought a two-story home on Fourth Avenue North and an adjacent building that became one of Birmingham's high-class brothels. Located near the police station, Lou and her "girls" were provided protection from violent patrons. Her wealth continued to grow.

Lou was adept not only at business but self-promotion as well. She reinvented herself, as some might say today. With her new wealth and position among Birmingham's elite came a new story to tell. Her father, according to this new version of herself, was a New Englander of "old Puritan stock," her mother was the daughter of a "wealthy southern planter" and she had been educated in fashionable boarding schools in aristocratic Mobile. After her mother's death when she was ten (she lowered her age from fifteen, presumably to make herself more sympathetic), a series of men claiming to be "gentlemen" betrayed her. Despite her attempts to enter polite society, she was not allowed to return from her "fall."

Lou's talent as a master storyteller led to a book chronicling her life titled *Autobiography of a Magdalene*. In the book, she claims she lived with a son of "one of Alabama's most important criminal lawyers" and then with a wealthy gentleman who lost his money gambling.

Perhaps her most outlandish claim was that she had an affair with John Wilkes Booth prior to his assassination of Abraham Lincoln. There's very little evidence to support her claim of a relationship with Booth. In 1890, Lou managed to persuade American newspapers, including the *Cincinnati Enquirer*, to report her belief that John Wilkes Booth was still alive. It is possible that they met, as Booth was in Montgomery between October and December 1860, appearing in a number of theatrical productions. He was quite the heartthrob of the day, and his performances were attended by many.

Lou retired in 1901 and eventually bought a house in what is now Birmingham's Southside, living with her sister and a nephew. While her name and much of her life story is known, there remains no known photo of the Birmingham madam.

When Lou died in 1913, local legend has it that Birmingham's prominent men sent empty carriages to her funeral, an act of both respect and anonymity. The parade of carriages was said to have stretched for blocks. In truth,

Tombstone of "Birmingham's Madam" Lou Wooster in Oak Hill Cemetery, 2012. *Photo by Beverly Crider.*

her burial was more likely a much quieter affair. According to at least one newspaper account, she was taken to her burial site practically unescorted.

There's also the rather doubtful idea that Margaret Mitchell based the character of Belle Watling in *Gone With the Wind* on Lou. Yet again, this is probably another example of truth and legend diverging. It's more likely that Mitchell based the Watling character on a madam from Lexington, Kentucky.

Lou is buried alongside her sister, also a Birmingham madam, and her nephew in a family plot on a hillside in Oak Hill Cemetery. Before her death, she bought plots adjacent to her own for proper and decent burials of other "women of the town" and also for other members of her staff who might otherwise have been dumped into graves in the paupers' field.

As is the case with so many legends, the actual truth about Lou Wooster may never be known. In this case, many believe it was Lou herself who created the legend. Her colorful character and her care for the sick and dying during the cholera epidemic of 1873 is what much of Birmingham chooses to remember. Had she not remained at that time, who's to say if Birmingham would have survived?

The Lou Wooster Public Health Award at the University of Alabama at Birmingham is named in her honor. The award is presented annually by the School of Public Health to recognize individuals, groups or organizations who are unconventional public health heroes. In 2000, Alabama Operaworks commissioned a work based on her life. *Louise: The*

Story of a Magdalen won the Nancy Van de Vate International Composition Prize for Opera in 2004.

Some of Lou's belongings are preserved among the Birmingham History Center's acquisitions. The collection includes a scrapbook that belonged to the madam, which contains newspaper clippings and handwritten notes.

CHAPTER 4

EDGAR CAYCE, THE SLEEPING PROPHET

E dgar Cayce (1877–1945), one of America's most celebrated psychics, was known as the "Sleeping Prophet" because he would close his eyes and appear to be in a self-induced trance during his readings. He is revered by hundreds of thousands of followers to this day. Often called the founder of the New Age movement, he spent more than a decade in Alabama.

Cayce (pronounced KAY-see) was born and raised in Hopkinsville, Kentucky, where he first reported seeing visions and speaking with the dead at age six. His religious parents were not shocked by his proclamation. In fact, they believed he had inherited his paternal grandfather's gift of "second sight." His grandfather Tom had been a well-known dowser, or "water witch," and was even said to have the power of telekinesis (the ability to move objects with his mind).

As is the case with so many legendary figures, it is difficult to determine where the truth ends and the legend begins. This is certainly true of Edgar Cayce. There are a few things that can be said for certain. He was a self-proclaimed "psychic diagnostician" who believed he had a God-given ability to heal the sick, and for forty-three years, he devoted his life to that cause.

Cayce's first experience with diagnostic healing took place in 1900, at the age of twenty-three. He had developed a severe case of laryngitis. At the time, he was working as a traveling insurance salesman trying to save money for his marriage to Gertrude Evans. He could barely speak above a whisper and had to quit this job due to his inability to communicate. He took a position as a photographer's assistant, which caused less strain on his vocal chords. When a hypnotist named Stanley "the Laugh King" Hart came to Hopkinsville, Edgar was ready to try anything to help end his laryngitis. The night of Hart's first performance, he hypnotized Edgar, who immediately began to speak with a clear voice during his trance. Upon waking, his laryngitis returned.

Later, at the suggestion of a New York osteopath, Cayce attempted a different type of hypnotism. Rather than instructing the sleeping Edgar to speak in a normal voice, he asked him to diagnose his own condition. As soon as Edgar went into a trance, he began describing his problem.

Edgar Cayce, the "Sleeping Prophet."

He was reported as saying under hypnosis, "This body is unable to speak due to partial paralysis of the inferior muscles of the vocal chords, produced by nerve strain. This is a psychological condition producing a physical effect."

Edgar went on to say the condition could be corrected by asking him to increase blood circulation to his throat. The suggestion worked, and when Edgar awoke, he was able to speak normally for the first time in almost a year. He claimed to have no memory of what occurred during the trance.

After his initial experiments with hypnosis, Cayce decided he could put his talents to use as a "spiritual healer." While under self-induced trances, he began diagnosing the health problems of poor, rural Kentuckians who couldn't afford the services of traditional doctors. During his trance, Edgar said he was able to place his mind in contact with a cosmic force that he called the "Source." Every reading ended with a prescribed treatment, many truly bizarre. He recommended "oil of smoke" (creosote made from pine tar) for a leg sore, "peach-tree poultice" for convulsions, "bedbug juice" for dropsy, "fumes of apple brandy from a charred keg" for tuberculosis and peanut oil rub to prevent arthritis. Many physicians in the area began to take issue with his claims of access to powers beyond science or reason.

Cayce's work grew in proportion to his fame. He asked for voluntary donations to support himself and his family so that he could practice full time. To help raise money, he invented Pit, a card game based on the commodities trading at the Chicago Board of Trade, and the game is still sold today.

Many people in the Kentucky community did not look favorably on Cayce's unorthodox healing methods. Arsonists burned Cayce's photography studios, forcing him to look for work outside the area. He found work as a traveling school photographer in Gadsden, Alabama. His work moved him from Gadsden to Anniston to Jacksonville to Montgomery. His reputation always followed.

In 1912, the H.P. Tressler Company offered Edgar a position in a portrait studio in Selma. There the Cayces settled into a quiet normalcy that suited Edgar. That calm was not to last, however. In 1914, his son Hugh Lynn was playing with flash power in Edgar's studio and severely burned his eyes. Doctors doubted the boy would ever see again and recommended removing his right eye. Edgar decided to give a reading on his son instead. He recommended that an additional compound be added to the solution the doctors prescribed and stated that Hugh Lynn should remain in a darkened room with his eyes bandaged for two weeks. After that period of time, when the bandages were removed, Hugh Lynn could see again.

Soon Cayce became even more famous, and he acquired more psychic business than photography business. For several months, he worked out of the Tutwiler Hotel in Birmingham. He also traveled out West, trying unsuccessfully to recruit investors to fund his psychic search for oil. He and his family finally left Alabama for good in 1923. Thereafter, Cayce's readings went beyond the diagnosis and treatment of illness to describe people's past lives, the experience of life after death and the true nature of Atlantis, of which he claimed to have once been a citizen.

Cayce suffered a stroke at the age of sixty-seven and died on January 3, 1945. The Edgar Cayce Association for Research and Enlightenment still operates out of Virginia Beach, Virginia.

CHAPTER 5

THE FIRST HUMAN INJURED BY A METEORITE

On November 30, 1954, an Alabama woman became the first human being ever injured by a meteorite. The now-famous "Hodges Meteorite," named for Ann E. Hodges, weighs about eight and a half pounds and is on permanent display at the Alabama Museum of Natural History at the University of Alabama.

Hodges was napping on a couch in her living room when the meteorite crashed through the ceiling of her home in the Oak Grove community near Sylacauga. Oddly enough, the house sat just across the road from the Comet Drive-In Theater, complete with a neon sign showing a comet streaking toward the heavens. The meteorite bounced off a radio console and smashed into her hip. She thought a gas heater had exploded. When she noticed a grapefruit-sized rock lying on the floor and a hole in the roof, she attributed it to mischievous children. Alabamians in and around the area reported seeing a fireball in the sky and heard a tremendous explosion. Most assumed an airplane had crashed.

Geologist George Swindel was conducting fieldwork in the area at the time and tentatively identified the object as a meteorite. It was turned over to officers from Maxwell Field in Montgomery, who took it to Air Force Intelligence authorities for analysis. After confirming it as a meteorite, they sent it to the Smithsonian Institution. Alabama congressman Kenneth Roberts had to intervene when the Smithsonian refused to return the meteorite to Alabama.

Television, radio and newspaper coverage lasted for weeks, highlighted by a very public dispute between the Hodgeses and Birdie Guy, who owned

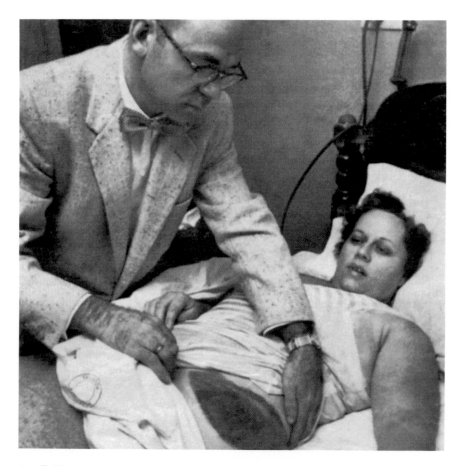

Ann E. Hodges, first human ever injured by a meteorite.

the home, in which the Hodgeses lived as renters. Facing repair expenses for the damaged house, Guy sued for possession of the rock. The Hodgeses threatened to countersue for Ann's injuries, and the outraged public sided with her. Before the case went to trial, the parties arrived at a modest private settlement, and Guy gave up her claim to the meteorite.

Hodges was featured in *Life* magazine and appeared on Gary Moore's TV quiz show *I've Got a Secret*, and her story appeared in the Sunday magazine supplement of many newspapers and in major magazines. Her husband, Hewlett Hodges, believed the couple stood to make a fortune from the incident. He refused what he considered an inadequate offer for the meteorite from the Smithsonian Institution. Hodges, not knowing how to bargain with the media, earned at most only a few hundred dollars from the

Hodges Meteorite, on display at the Alabama Museum of Natural History on the University of Alabama campus in Tuscaloosa, 2012. *Photo by Beverly Crider.*

incident that had made her famous. By 1956, the bad publicity surrounding the lawsuit ended the monetary offers, and she donated the meteorite to the Alabama Museum of Natural History, where it remains.

What makes this story even more amazing is that meteorites typically fall into the ocean or strike one of Earth's vast, remote places, according to Michael Reynolds, a Florida State College astronomer and author of the book *Falling Stars: A Guide to Meteors & Meteorites.*

"Think of how many people have lived throughout human history," Reynolds said. "You have a better chance of getting hit by a tornado and a bolt of lightning and a hurricane all at the same time."

Although Ann recovered from her physical injuries, the brush with celebrity put such a strain on the Hodgeses' marriage that they separated in 1964. Ann's health declined, and in 1972, after some years as an invalid, she died.

While the major players in this historical event ended up wishing the whole thing had never happened, a farmer who lived down the road, Julius McKinney, made a small fortune behind the scenes. The day after the meteorite fell to Earth, McKinney was driving his wagon when his mules shied away from a black rock in the road. Geologists confirmed that he had found a smaller piece of the same meteorite. McKinney sold his three-and-a-half-pound rock to the Smithsonian, where it resides today in the Hall of Meteorites. Strangely, the labeling on this fragment does not mention its more famous Alabama sibling. McKinney made enough from the sale to purchase a small farm and a used car.

On May 22, 2010, what is now the town of Oak Grove dedicated a historical marker at the site of the meteorite strike. In honor of the occasion, the Alabama Museum of Natural History, located on the University of Alabama campus in Tuscaloosa, sent the meteorite to the town for the day as part of the festivities.

As the historic marker reads, "The Hodges and McKinney Aerolites are the only known meteors from that day but other 'comets' surely reached the ground the day 'Stars Fell on Alabama.'"

CHAPTER 6

THE GOAT MAN

He wrestled a bear, narrowly avoided being lynched by the Ku Klux Klan, was pronounced dead and taken to the morgue, became an ordained preacher and even got mugged in Los Angeles while trying to see actress Morgan Fairchild—or so the story goes.

Charles "Chess" McCartney was his name, but most people knew him only as the "Goat Man." He was one of the South's most famous wandering travelers and folk characters.

McCartney was born in Iowa and was believed to be 97 when he died in 1998, but he was rumored to be as old as 120. No one really knows. The main sources for biographical information about McCartney are McCartney himself and his son. Some of the often-colorful details vary.

The adventures began when McCartney was fourteen and ran away from his farm and settled in New York. There he married a Spanish knife-thrower ten years his senior. He served as her target for a couple years before returning to Iowa to farm. When that failed at the beginning of the Depression, he went to work for the Works Progress Administration (WPA) cutting trees. After a timbering tree shattered his left side, he was pronounced dead, only to awaken on a shocked undertaker's table.

McCartney had always been fond of goats since his days on the family farm, and after his timbering accident, he came up with the idea of using a goat cart to travel with his family and work as an itinerant preacher.

His wife did not like the idea and left, according to one account. Another says that his wife and son joined him, and his wife even made goatskin clothes

The Goat Man.

for McCartney and his son to wear as a gimmick on their travels. She quickly grew tired of the road and returned to Iowa. Some variations on the story say she took their son with her; others say he remained with the Goat Man. Yet another version of the tale says that McCartney sold his wife to another farmer for $1,000. He was said to have married at least two more times.

McCartney's iron-wheeled wagon was large, rickety and covered with objects he found along the road. It held a bed, a potbellied stove, lanterns, pots, pans, car tags and assorted sundries. His traveling goat herd sometimes numbered up to thirty. From 1930 to 1987, legend has it, McCartney walked 100,000 miles, preaching the Gospel in forty-nine states and Canada before retiring in the late 1960s after he was beaten and robbed one night near Chattanooga, Tennessee.

McCartney died in 1998 in a Georgia nursing home. No one is sure how many of his stories actually happened, but numerous people have personal memories of the man or have heard tales of him from others. Whatever he was in life, he is a folklore legend in death.

CHAPTER 7

ANNISTON'S JAMES BOND

B erman. Farley Berman.
    The name might not be as famous as that of the iconic spy of the big screen, but a spy he was. In fact, Farley met his wife, Germaine, also a spy, while they were spying on each other during World War II. Did you get all that?

When the war was over, the couple settled in Farley's hometown of Anniston, Alabama. The couple kept their heads down, running a women's clothing store and spending the next forty years traveling the globe for "collectibles."

Their collection became the Berman Museum of World History in 1996. While it displays everything from rare books to "Arts of Asia," its centerpiece has always been Farley's collection of weapons and war memorabilia. Somehow he managed to acquire everything from poison arrows to battle-axes and grenade launchers to a launch control panel for a V-2 rocket, according to a report on the Roadside America website.

The museum displays World War II German rifles with bent barrels that could shoot around corners and an executioner's axe from England that, according to Farley, chopped off seventy-five heads. Among Farley's collection are belt buckles that fire bullets, exploding cigarette lighters, Jefferson Davis's traveling pistols, a jeweled dagger that belonged to the Egyptian King Faurok and a scimitar of Abbas the Great of Persia. The highlight of the World War II collection is not a weapon, however, but the silver tea service of Adolph Hitler. (Hitler's typewriter is a couple hours away at the Bessemer Hall of History Museum.)

A member of the U.S. Army Counter Intelligence Corps during World War II, Farley remained tight-lipped about how he managed to track down many of his finds. According to a 2008 *Anniston Star* article, when people asked about his artifacts, Farley would respond, "I don't know. It just showed up in my bedroom this morning."

The Berman Museum's collection of "combination" and assassination weapons is purportedly equal to that of the International Spy Museum in Washington, D.C. The twenty-five-thousand-square-foot facility also includes exhibits on the American West and an array of artwork by such artists as Rodin, Remington and Toulouse-Lautrec. One of the more amazing acquisitions in the Berman holdings is a royal scimitar dating from 1587 that belonged to Abbas I of Persia. The sword is ornamented with 1,295 rose-cut diamonds and many other precious gems, which are set in three pounds of gold. Published reports have valued the collection at $100 million.

Farley died in 1999 at the age of eighty-eight.

CHAPTER 8

WHERE NO MAN (OR WOMAN) HAS GONE BEFORE

I n the late 1960s, as the Starship Enterprise was starting its "Wagon Train to the Stars," Birmingham's Loulie Jean Norman was sending the crew off on their five-year mission with her stellar coloratura soprano voice. She provided the voice behind one of the most recognized themes on television, the ethereal opening to the original *Star Trek* series. Sadly, she only received studio pay for a one-time gig for the song.

Born on March 12, 1913, in Birmingham, Alabama, Norman graduated from Phillips High School, where she was a classmate of Hugh Martin, the composer perhaps best known for writing "Have Yourself a Merry Little Christmas." The two became close friends.

Norman began her career as a radio singer and model in New York City. She performed with

Loulie Jean Norman provided the coloratura soprano voice behind the opening to the original *Star Trek* television series.

Mel Tormé's Mel Tones; dubbed the singing voice for Diahann Carroll's character, Clara, in the 1959 film version of *Porgy and Bess*; and sang backup vocals on Elvis Presley's "Moonlight Swim" from the *Blue Hawaii* soundtrack. Her soprano vocals also can be heard on the Tokens' 1961 hit "The Lion Sleeps Tonight."

She was one of the original Ray Coniff Singers in the 1960s and appeared on the Dean Martin, Carol Burnett and Dinah Shore television shows. She sang with many of the great vocalists of the era, including Frank Sinatra, Bing Crosby, Ray Charles, Spike Jones, Frankie Laine and Henry Mancini.

After her vocals on the *Star Trek* theme, perhaps her most recognizable performance is that of the Crazy Ghost in Disney Theme Park's "Haunted Mansion" attraction.

Norman had four children with her husband, Norman Henry Price. She died in 2005 at her home in Studio City, California.

CHAPTER 9

TURN ON, TUNE IN, DROP OUT!

Timothy Leary is probably best known as a counterculture icon of the 1960s. He was a writer, psychologist and advocate for the use of psychoactive drugs. If you don't recognize his name, you might recognize the phrase he coined: "Turn on, tune in, drop out."

Leary, born on October 22, 1920, in Springfield, Massachusetts, attended the University of Alabama, where he studied psychology. He was expelled in 1942 for spending the night in a women's dormitory. He was later reinstated after a brief service in the Army Medical Corps in Pennsylvania and allowed to complete his degree requirements by correspondence.

After receiving master's and doctoral degrees, Leery became a professor of psychology and a leading member of the American drug culture of the 1960s, promoting psychedelic drugs such as lysergic acid diethylamide (LSD). His mantra, "Turn on, tune in, drop out," became one of the most recognized slogans of the movement. Many interpreted the phrase to mean "get stoned and abandon all constructive activity," he later wrote. "'Turn on' meant go within to activate your neural and genetic equipment. Drugs were one way to accomplish this end. 'Tune in' meant interact harmoniously with the world around you. 'Drop out' meant self-reliance, a discovery of one's singularity."

Alabama had another brush with counterculture fame when British psychiatrist Humphrey Osmond joined the faculty at the University of Alabama School of Medicine. Like Timothy Leary, Osmond spent much of his career researching hallucinogenic drugs. In fact, it was Osmond who coined the phrase "psychedelic" to describe them.

Timothy Leary, 1960s counterculture icon.

Osmond began researching schizophrenia while serving with John R. Smythies in the Royal Navy during World War II. Posted at St. George's Hospital in London, the colleagues developed a theory that schizophrenia was caused by production of LSD-like compounds in the brain. After the war, they took their research to Saskatchewan Hospital in Canada, where they asserted that the use of the hallucinogen mescaline could induce short-term schizophrenia, thus giving doctors a chance to more closely study the condition and gain better insight into its effects.

"Psychedelic" poster.

One of the study participants was novelist Aldous Huxley, author of 1931's *Brave New World*, which described a totalitarian society in which the population is controlled by drugs. Although Osmond had used the term "psychedelic" to describe hallucinogens in technical reports, it was through his correspondence with Huxley that the term became widely known.

As they searched for a name to describe hallucinogenic drugs, Huxley proposed the word "phanerothyme," derived from roots relating to "spirit" or "soul." He wrote to Osmond, "To make this trivial world sublime/Take half a gramme of phanerothyme." Osmond replied: "To fathom hell or soar angelic/Just take a pinch of psychedelic."

Osmond left Saskatchewan for the New Jersey Psychiatric Institute in Princeton. From there, he became a professor of psychology at the University of Alabama School of Medicine, practicing at Bryce State Mental Hospital in Tuscaloosa. His former colleague John Smythies was then teaching at the Birmingham campus of the school, and the two renewed their work. When the use of hallucinogenic drugs in research was outlawed, Osmond began researching the use of large doses of vitamins in psychiatric treatment.

After the founding of the University of Alabama at Birmingham (UAB), Osmond became a psychology professor there, again researching schizophrenia. I guess you could say Alabama played a big role in the "dawning of the Age of Aquarius," man.

CHAPTER 10

HOLY SMOKES, BIRMINGHAM...IT'S BATMAN!

Birmingham residents of the 1970s and '80s were living alongside a true superhero, and some may never have known it. The "Birmingham Batman," Willie James Perry, was not in it for the glory, and he did not toot his own horn, so to speak. He was, however, known to help stranded motorists with free rides in his customized 1971 Ford Thunderbird, dubbed the "Batmobile Rescue Ship."

Birmingham Batman, born in 1941, was known around town for helping people in need. He lived by the Golden Rule and made sure he had extra gas, a tool case and jumper cables in his car just in case he came across a motorist in distress. He gave free rides to anyone who may have had a bit too much to drink, helped the elderly make it to their doctor appointments and even took kids for rides in his Batmobile.

His ride was equipped with running water, a toaster oven, a television, a "computerized" phone, twelve audio speakers, a soda fountain dispenser, strobe lights, a microwave oven and a stereo. Holy smokes! Remember, it was the early '80s! It also carried forty-eight-inch red fluorescent lights on both sides, yellow lights in the back and two revolving lights on the hood and featured orange shag carpeting.

The Batmobile Rescue Ship was even featured on the television show *That's Incredible!* When the Jacksons' tour brought them to Birmingham, Michael Jackson spotted the car and had his limo driver pull over so he could examine the Batmobile.

According to a 1982 United Press International (UPI) article, one beneficiary of Perry's kindness was Dorothy Clark and her five children, who found themselves on the side of the interstate with a flat tire. Clark was taking her children to the park when the tire blew.

> *"The guy jumped out and showed me his Batman identification card and offered to take us to the park. I thought, 'This is really weird,' but I said, 'I've got to trust someone.'"*
>
> *At the end of the day he picked the family up at the park, returned them to the car, put on a new tire and set them on their way.*
>
> *"I tried to give him money, but he wouldn't take it. He said, 'No, you just be careful,' and he drove away."*

Perry died of carbon monoxide poisoning while he was working on the Batmobile in 1985. The garage doors had apparently closed unnoticed.

CHAPTER 11

THE HEAVIEST MEMBER
OF CONGRESS

Back in the first half of the nineteenth century, Alabama had the distinction of being the state with the largest representation in Congress, according to the jokes around Washington. Dixon Hall Lewis, a U.S senator from Lowndes County, Alabama, was an early states' rights advocate, but he was probably best known for being the heaviest member of Congress, reportedly weighing around 430 pounds.

Special chairs had to be constructed to accommodate his girth. He gave speeches sitting down because standing for lengthy periods of time was too difficult for him. Lewis required his aides to constantly fan him, as any exertion tired him and caused him to sweat profusely. He had to travel in custom-built carriages. On one occasion, Lewis's extreme weight caused him to fall through the floor of a stagecoach as he traveled through Georgia.

During his tenure in Washington, Lewis became something of a tourist attraction. "One might as well visit St. Petersburg without obtaining a view of the Autocrat of all the Russias, as sojourn, however briefly, at the capital of the United States, without a sight of the great Southern member," one contemporary wrote.

Despite the jokes, Lewis proved to be a gifted orator and served in both the U.S. House of Representatives and the U.S. Senate.

Throughout most of his life, Lewis maintained a good humor about his weight. As the years passed, however, he found the jokes less funny. It was said he refused to be weighed near the end of his life. It was his obesity that finally caused his demise. He died on October 25, 1848, at the age of forty-six, in

Dixon Hall Lewis, a U.S senator from Lowndes County, Alabama, was probably best known for being the heaviest member of Congress, reportedly weighing around 430 pounds.

New York City, where he had gone to seek medical advice. Transporting his body home proved to be problematic, so the staunch southerner was buried in Brooklyn. To honor Lewis, the mayor of New York held a public funeral at city hall.

CHAPTER 12

RUBE BURROW

ROBIN HOOD OR KING OF THE OUTLAWS?

He might not have been as famous as Jesse James, but Alabama's Rube Burrow (also known as Rube Burrows) was dubbed "King of the Outlaws" by a number of publications of the late 1880s, becoming the most feared train robber of the time. His exploits were legendary, and several books were written about his life. An Emmy-winning television series by Republic Pictures in 1954–55 featured accounts of Jesse James, Billy the Kid, Black Bart, Doc Holliday and Rube Burrow. In 1966, Leaf issued bubble gum cards of the most famous "Bad Guys." Burrow was included.

One of ten children, Burrow was born in 1855 near the town of Sulligent in Lamar County, where his father worked as a farmer and schoolteacher. His mother was known in the area as Dame Burrow, a faith healer and "witch," supposedly curing cancers by simple incantation. As boys, Rube and his younger brother Jim were enthralled by tales of outlaw Jesse James and his gang. According to some accounts, Burrow, wearing a mask, robbed a neighbor at gunpoint at the age of fifteen. His father recognized him and made him return the money.

In the early to mid-1870s, he moved to Texas to work as a hand on his Uncle Joel's cattle ranch, and his brother Jim joined him in 1876. There, Rube married Virginia Alvison, daughter of prominent Wise County rancher H.B. Alvison. The couple had two children before Virginia died in 1880. Rube sent his children back to Alabama with his brother, and he remained in Texas, where he remarried. That relationship was not to last.

Sketch depicting a Rube Burrow shootout.

Burrow became more restless over time, and still inspired by tales of Jesse James, he robbed his first train in Texas in 1886. At least eight more train robberies followed in Texas, Arkansas, Alabama and Mississippi. He murdered the postmaster in Jewel, Alabama. His gang, which included his brother Jim, remained small. Robberies were usually committed by Burrow and only one or two accomplices.

Some Rube Burrow legends have glossed over his more heinous crimes and made the train robber into more of an "Alabama Robin Hood" because he allegedly never robbed the poor. No real evidence exists to support that claim, however. The majority of his robberies targeted the U.S. Postal Service and rail companies.

Adding to his Robin Hood persona is the tale of Burrow's aid to a widow who gave him a free meal when he was hungry. While he ate his dinner, the widow told Burrow of a $700 mortgage on her property that was past due. She said the banker would arrive at any moment to foreclose. Burrow gave the widow the $700, telling her to make sure she got a receipt. He then waited in the nearby woods and met the banker as he was leaving, recovering his money.

The gang's luck began to run out in Nashville, Tennessee, when a conductor spotted the Burrow brothers on a train pulling into the station. Lawmen trapped Rube and Jim in a passenger car. Rube managed to escape, but Jim was jailed in Texarkana, where he died of consumption on October 5, 1888.

With "Wanted" posters everywhere, Burrow became the subject of one of America's most widespread manhunts. Burrow continued robbing trains, returning to Alabama when he needed the protection of the locals. It was a local, however, who proved to be his undoing. And here the story, once again, has multiple variations from which to choose.

In early October 1890, Linden store owner Jefferson Davis "Dixie" Carter recognized Burrow. In some accounts, Carter captured the outlaw, locking him in a storeroom while he went in search of police. Burrow escaped and, instead of fleeing, went in search of Carter in retaliation. Rube spotted the shopkeeper at the train depot, opened fire and shot Carter in the arm. Carter drew his own weapon, shooting Burrow in the stomach. The outlaw died in the street.

In a different account, Burrow was arrested and had not been in custody for half a day when he attempted escape. He made his way to the front of the jail, where he engaged Carter in a shootout. Burrow fired all of his bullets, hitting Carter once in the abdomen. Carter then shot Burrow in the chest, killing him instantly.

In yet a different account, Carter recognized Burrow and had him arrested, only for Burrow to escape a short time later. Rather than fleeing town, Burrow went to confront Carter. A gunfight erupted, and Carter

Rube Burrow in his casket as he was shown at railroad stops along the ride back to his native Alabama.

was shot in the arm. Carter chased Burrow from a feed store and, with the aid of John McDuffie, gunned him down in the street.

The one thing they all have in common: Carter killed Burrow.

Rube Burrow's body was shipped by train back to Lamar County, making several stops along the way so that the public could see the body of the famous train robber. His weapons were also put on display in Memphis, Tennessee, and attracted huge crowds. It was reported that at a stop in Birmingham, thousands viewed the corpse, and people snatched buttons from his coat, cut hair from his head and even took his boots. Burrow's father met the train in Sulligent. It was reported that the train attendants threw the coffin at his feet. Allen Burrow carried his son's body back to his home community near Vernon and buried him in Fellowship Cemetery.

CHAPTER 13

THE LEGEND OF RENA TEEL

I rene "Rena" Vansandt was born with a caul over her head on April 8, 1894, near the town of Rockford in Coosa County. The midwife who assisted at her birth screamed when she saw the covering over the baby's head. According to superstitions of the time, babies born with a veil, or caul, have a "sixth sense"—they are able to foretell the future. Some cultures even associated it with witchcraft. Today, we know it simply means she was born with her amniotic sac intact, which poses no risk to the infant.

Aside from being born with the caul, Rena seemed to be a healthy baby girl, and her mother soon began to relax. Eventually, however, Rena's "talents" began to manifest themselves. She was able to locate missing objects and was even able to tell the locals what the future had in store for them.

Once, when Rena was twelve, she tearfully told her mother that her infant brother George was going to die. Because the baby was healthy, her mother didn't take the warning seriously. Three days later, George died.

Rena was a deeply religious woman, and she dreaded the notoriety that followed the public discovery of her psychic powers. She feared the public would misunderstand what she had begun to consider a gift from God. She attempted to separate herself from the traditional image of a fortuneteller.

On October 6, 1912, Rena married Ben Teel in her family's Coosa County log home and eventually gave birth to a baby boy, James. In October 1914, Ben woke to find Rena in tears. She had dreamed that while visiting her parents, they asked about baby James, and she told them, "I have no baby." Rena worried that history was repeating itself. Like her baby brother George so many years earlier, James seemed perfectly healthy. But nine days later, he was dead. The Teels would go on to have two healthy children, Marvin Pruet and Dollie Irene.

By 1917, the Teels had moved to Millerville. Initially, Rena read primarily for individuals on the fringes of society, such as bootleggers and convicts, and she resisted any sort of advertising. She preferred to be available as a neighborly advocate for those in need. Eventually, however, her clientele began to grow and even included prestigious members of the community. She began setting up appointments and accepting donations—usually ten to fifty cents. Cars of her clients began crowding the yard, and somebody reported her for not having a business license. Rena had not known one was necessary but obtained one immediately and kept it the rest of her life.

One of the most notable accounts of Rena's "gift" occurred in Talladega. Upon seeing a hangman's scaffold, she immediately knew a terrible mistake was about to take place. The man to be hanged was innocent; she just "knew" it. The case involved a rape, and the victim had sworn the convicted man was her rapist. Rena's friend convinced her to stay out of the matter. Rena did as her friend advised but said that within two years the true rapist would confess. The execution went forward, and two years later, the uncle of the wrongfully executed man confessed to the crime on his deathbed.

John Williams of *Like the Dew, a Journal of Southern Culture and Politics* related his own family tale of "Mrs. Rena," as she became known:

In 1950, my mother and her new mother-in-law, my…grandmother, made [a] trip from Montgomery to Clay County to consult Rena Teel. Her pronouncements of that day apparently weren't sensational enough to live on in family lore. Except for one thing. My newlywed parents' house at that time, on Lewis Street in Montgomery, had a back porch which had been converted to a sort of sun room, its three exterior walls entirely windows. Mama had made a laundry room of it. A lover of flowers, she had had my father build for her around the inside of those spacious, sunny windows a series of glass shelves for her collection of African violets and other exotic blooming plants. Rena Teel described the room, the shelves, the plants, with minute accuracy. But she added that some catastrophe was in store for them, and that they would all be lost, save one.

One day a few weeks later, as the washing machine went into the spin cycle and began to shake the porch, as it always did, my mother, in another room, suddenly heard a thunderous, horrible, multi-staged crash. She rushed into the laundry room to find a scene of devastation—shattered glass, broken pottery, dirt, gravel, plants. In one window, a single small potted African violet still stood.

In Clay County, it became a sort of rite of passage to visit Mrs. Rena down in Millerville. Former Alabama first lady Patsy Riley joined her two best friends during their senior year in high school to participate in that rite. She wrote in a 2009 *Alabama Heritage* article that she was already in love with the future governor, Bob Riley, and was there to hear Mrs. Rena confirm her choice.

Mrs. Teel sat by a large window. She told me I would have three children. She told me I would marry a man who was at least two heads taller than I was. She told me red or reddish hair was in my future, a child or a husband. She told me one day I would own lots and lots of land. If I sold the land, she said that I shouldn't sell the mineral rights to that large amount of land I'd own one day. She also told me I would be happy no matter where I lived.

I did marry a man two heads taller (not hard since I'm 5'3"). One of my grandchildren had reddish hair as a baby. My grandfather was also redhead. I do own a large amount of land, and our farm is sitting where graphite once was mined. I have four children, now three; however three are with me in body and soul. One lives with Jesus, and she is with me in spirit and soul.

Rena Teel died on May 14, 1964, after a long battle with cancer. Several years later, family friend Ammie Anderson published *Irene Vansandt Teel*, a brief biography that collected anecdotes, accolades and accounts of Rena's accomplishments. Aside from this small, rare volume and assorted newspaper articles, few recorded accounts exist of Mrs. Rena and her skills.

CHAPTER 14

THE ALABAMIANS WHO PROVED HITLER WRONG

The son of an Alabama sharecropper and grandson of a slave accomplished more than any Olympian before him at the 1936 Summer Olympic Games.

Winning four gold medals, Jesse Owens did more than win at sports: he trampled Adolf Hitler's plans to use the Olympics as a showcase for the talents of his "superior" Aryan race. He won the gold medal in the one-hundred-meter with a 10.3-second time, tying the world record. He continued by winning the gold medal in the long jump with 26 feet, 5.25 inches, a new Olympic record, and winning the gold medal in the two-hundred-meter with a 20.7-second time, also a new Olympic record. Finally, Jesse, Ralph Metcalfe, Foy Draper and Frank Wykoff won the gold medal in the four-by-one-hundred relay with a time of 39.8 seconds, setting a new world record.

The youngest of ten children, James Cleveland (J.C.) was born to Henry and Emma Owens in Oakville, Alabama. A small child, he was sick with pneumonia for weeks at a time. He also developed dangerous boils on his chest and legs. Unable to afford medical care, his father held the crying child while his mother carved the boils out of his flesh with a red-hot kitchen knife. By the age of six, J.C. was well enough to walk the nine miles to school with his brothers and sisters.

He recalled that even though he was thin and sickly, "I always loved running. I wasn't very good at it, but I loved it because it was something you could do all by yourself, and under your own power. You could go any direction, as fast or as slow as you wanted, fighting the wind if you felt like it, seeking out new sights just on the strength of your feet and the courage of your lungs."

J.C. was nine years old when his family moved to Cleveland, Ohio, in search of better work opportunities. In 1923, he enrolled at Bolton Elementary School. When his teacher asked for J.C.'s name, she misunderstood his southern accent and wrote Jesse. Afraid to interrupt on the first day of class, J.C. became Jesse, a name that stuck with him for the rest of his life.

Throughout his life, Jesse attributed the success of his athletic career to the encouragement of Charles Riley, his junior high track coach at Fairmount Junior High School.

He said, "Every morning, just like in Alabama, I got up with the sun, ate my breakfast even before my mother and sisters and brothers, and went to school, winter, spring, and fall alike to run and jump and bend my body this way and that for Mr. Charles Riley."

In his first year on his track team, Jesse broke the world record for junior high in the high jump and long jump. He led his team to the state championship in May 1931 and then again in May 1932, when Jesse equaled or broke records in the long jump, the one-hundred- and two-hundred-yard sprints and the relay event.

U.S. gold medalist Jesse Owens talks to German silver medalist Luz Long at the 1936 Olympic Games in Berlin.

Jesse enrolled at Ohio State University (OSU) in September 1933 after employment was found for his father, ensuring that the family could be supported. OSU had only one men's dormitory, which did not permit black athletes, so Jesse and his black teammates were forced to live in a house off campus. When he traveled with the team, Jesse was restricted to ordering carryout or eating at "black-only" restaurants and had to stay at "black-only" hotels. He did not receive a scholarship for his efforts, so he continued to work part-time jobs to pay for school.

Known as the "Buckeye bullet," Jesse won a record eight individual NCAA championships, four each in 1935 and 1936. (The record of four gold medals at the NCAA was equaled only by Xavier Carter in 2006, although his many titles also included relay medals.)

After completing his athletic career, Jesse supported his young family with a variety of jobs. One was of special significance: playground director in Cleveland. It was his first step into a lifetime of working with underprivileged youth. After relocating to Chicago, he spent much of his time as a board member and former director of the Chicago Boys' Club.

"We all have dreams," Jesse said. "In order to make dreams come into reality, it takes an awful lot of determination, dedication, self-discipline and effort."

In tribute to the greatest track and field athlete of all time, the Jesse Owens Memorial Park was dedicated in Jesse's hometown of Oakville on June 29, 1996, with the arrival of the Olympic torch en route to the XXVI Olympic Games in Atlanta.

More than ten thousand people from across the country attended the dedication ceremony. Stuart Owen Rankin, Jesse's grandson, carried the Olympic torch into the park. One of the greatest moments of the day was the unveiling of the Jesse Owens statue in the Gold Medallion Court located just outside the park's museum.

The statue depicts Owens bursting through the Olympic rings. Birmingham sculptor Branko Medenica designed the statue to represent all the barriers that Owens broke in becoming an Olympic hero. The statue's inscription reads: "Athlete and humanitarian whose inspiration personifies the spirit and promise of America."

Owens was not the only Alabamian to prove Hitler wrong in his quest to prove Aryan supremacy. The son of a LaFayette sharecropper, great-grandson of a slave and great-great-grandson of a white slave owner, Joe Louis rose up through the ranks of amateur and professional boxing to become the world heavyweight champion, a title he held from 1937 to

Jesse Owens statue in the Gold Medallion Court, located just outside the Jesse Owens Memorial Park in the athlete's hometown of Oakville, 2012. *Photo by Beverly Crider.*

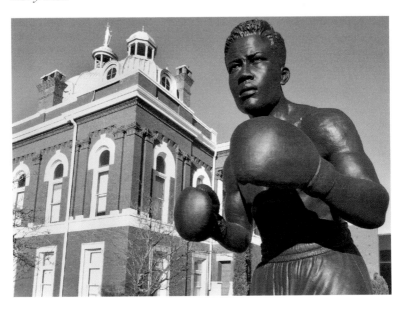

Statue of boxing great Joe Louis located in Joe's hometown of LaFayette, Alabama. The statue is located in Courthouse Square in front of the new Chambers County Courthouse annex. *Wikimedia Commons.*

Image of Joe Louis on U.S. postage stamp.

1949. Louis (known as the "Brown Bomber") is perhaps best known for his legendary matchups against German boxer Max Schmeling.

After Schmeling defeated Louis in their first bout in 1936, their rematch in 1938 took on worldwide importance as the press portrayed the match as an epic battle between Nazi ideology and American democratic ideals (even though Schmeling was never a member of the Nazi Party). There were reports that Hitler warned Schmeling that he had better win for the glory of the Third Reich. When Louis defeated Schmeling by a knockout in the first round, Louis became an American hero.

Louis spent his last four years in a wheelchair before dying of a heart attack at sixty-six on April 12, 1981, in Las Vegas. He was buried in Arlington National Cemetery at the request of President Ronald Reagan.

An eight-foot bronze statue of the "Brown Bomber," sculpted by Casey Downing Jr., is on display in Louis's hometown of LaFayette. Residents of the town of approximately three thousand people managed to raise nearly $60,000 over a span of three years to pay for the sculpture. The statue, which has a base of Alabama red granite, was erected outside the Chambers County Courthouse.

CHAPTER 15

JOHN HENRY, THE STEEL DRIVIN' MAN

If ever there were a tale to compete with those of Pecos Bill or Paul Bunyan, it would be that of John Henry, the "Steel Drivin' Man." And while Georgia, Virginia or West Virginia might like to lay claim to him, we Alabamians know he drove that railroad spike right here at an Oak Mountain tunnel near Leeds.

Did ol' Henry really exist, or is he just a tall tale that incorporates the dreams and ideals of a struggling new nation? There are many references throughout the years that would suggest that he was, indeed, a real railroad worker. There is little hard evidence about the facts of his life, but the general consensus is that he was a former slave who helped construct the railroads in the late 1800s. He was one of thousands of men hired by railroad companies to smooth out terrain and cut through obstacles that stood in the way of proposed tracks.

According to a National Public Radio special featuring Henry, "His tale has become the stuff of myth. He has embodied the spirit of growth in America for over a century." He has been the subject of novels, a postage stamp and even animated films. Above all, "John Henry" is the single most well-known and often-recorded American folk song.

Railroad workers used large hammers and stakes to pound holes into the rock, which were then filled with explosives that would blast the opening deeper and deeper into the mountain. Tunnel engineers were beginning to use steam drills to break through rock at a faster pace. John Henry, upon hearing of this new machine, challenged the steam drill to a contest. He won but died of exhaustion.

Image on John Henry postage stamp.

Many early John Henry ballads feature the blasting of the Big Bend Tunnel—more than a mile through a mountain in West Virginia. Some John Henry experts believe it was unlikely that Henry was at that tunnel. They believe he raced a steam drill at Oak Mountain in Alabama during the 1880s. In fact, there is popular local lore around Leeds, Alabama, that John

Historical marker honoring John Henry, the "Steel Drivin' Man," at the depot in Leeds, Alabama, 2013. *Photo by Beverly Crider.*

Henry raced the drill just outside the east portal of Oak Mountain Tunnel, between Oak and Coosa Mountain Tunnels. In about a dozen versions of "John Henry," there are lines that are more consistent with the Alabama location than with the West Virginia site.

Excerpts from the journal of E.L. Voyles, a road superintendent for the Seaboard Air Line Railroad during the early twentieth century, claim that trains passing through the Oak Mountain Tunnel would blow their steam whistles to honor John Henry.

As is the case with so many legends, especially those popular in a time before every action was easily photographed and documented online, we may never know the exact details of John Henry's race with a steam drill. We just know it took place in Alabama.

CHAPTER 16

SUN RA, ALABAMA'S VISITOR FROM SATURN

Herman Blount, a Birmingham jazz musician who later became known as Sun Ra, was an eccentric music visionary who claimed he was a visitor from the planet Saturn. Born in 1914, young Herman was not only a musical prodigy but showed great promise in academic pursuits as well. He attended Alabama A&M University in Huntsville for a brief time but left to pursue a career in music. It was at this time in the late 1930s that he first claimed that he had been abducted by a UFO that took him to Saturn.

He returned to Birmingham, where he became one of the first proponents of electronic music, purchasing an electric keyboard when they became available. Later in his life, he was among the first to use synthesizers and was one of the first jazz leaders to use the electric bass. He received a Minimoog (monophonic analog synthesizer) prototype from inventor Robert Moog.

Blount became a conscientious objector during World War II and spent time in jail and at a civilian public service camp in Pennsylvania before being released in 1943 due to poor health. He moved to Chicago in 1946 and in 1952 officially changed his name to Le'Sony'r Ra and began to distance himself from Alabama and the South. He eventually left his old persona behind and took on that of a somewhat mythical being of his own creation. He was known by several variations of Le'Sony'r Ra, but he was known by most as simply "Sun Ra," Ra being the Egyptian god of the sun.

Combining aspects of both outer space and ancient Egypt into his personal and theatrical mythology, Sun Ra was not easy to categorize, although he has become quite a legend in the jazz world. In the civil rights era, his band

Sun Ra, Alabama's visitor from Saturn.

proudly celebrated black history and combined it with the possibilities of space travel. He was interested in many religions and the occult and was especially drawn to Egyptian culture.

Sun Ra's interest in language and wordplay led to his selection of the name for his band, the Arkestra. While the band took shape in the mid- to late 1950s, the band underwent many name changes, but the term Arkestra was a part of many. Sun Ra combined the word "orchestra" and the word "Ark," used both in the Old Testament's Ark of the Covenant as well as referring to the ark that transported the Egyptian god Ra. The term Arkestra represented a new approach in the jazz world. Not only did the group combine a collection of musicians, but it also encompassed multifaceted performance art and a mythological world.

The band performed in long robes made of decorated metallic fabric and wore elaborate headpieces inspired by Egyptian costume. Some headpieces represented cosmic themes. Dancers dressed in costumes reminiscent of science fiction, and their performances were accompanied by light shows. The group recorded more than one hundred records, with some members staying only a few months and others staying for decades.

In late 1968, Sun Ra and his Arkestra made their first trip to the West Coast. There they often played for a younger crowd who were somewhat taken aback by the large ensemble that had grown to include twenty to thirty musicians, dancers and fire-eaters and theatrical lighting. By 1969, however, Sun Ra was on the cover of *Rolling Stone* magazine.

Sun Ra's health began to deteriorate in the early 1990s, and he returned to Birmingham to be with his family. He died on May 30, 1993, of pneumonia. He is buried in Elmwood Cemetery in Birmingham, where a small footstone reads "Herman Blount (aka Le Son'y Ra)."

CHAPTER 17

VIRGINIA HILL, MISTRESS OF BUGSY SIEGEL

According to Mark Gribben of TruTV, "No woman personified the mob girlfriend more than Virginia Hill, aka the Flamingo." A Lipscomb, Alabama native, Virginia moved to Marietta, Georgia, with her mother and two brothers in the 1930s. She left Georgia in her teens and headed to Chicago, where she became a dancer at the World's Fair. Around the time of her seventeenth birthday, Virginia began working at the San Carlo Italian Village restaurant, a favorite meeting place of Al Capone's mob.

Eventually, she became the mistress of Chicago Outfit mobsters Frank Costello, Frank Nitti, Charles Fischetti and Joe Adonis. She was, reportedly, a "bag woman," who funneled outfit funds into Swiss bank accounts. By August 1938, she was in Hollywood, California, where Benjamin "Bugsy" Siegel was in charge of the organized crime scene.

Less than a year after her arrival in California, Virginia met former University of Alabama football player Osgood Griffin at a bar. They were engaged that same night and married soon after, but the marriage was annulled after only six months. Virginia began seeing Bugsy during the 1940s and eventually became his most favored mistress. Bugsy called Virginia the "Flamingo," supposedly because of her long legs. Many believe that the Las Vegas "Flamingo Hotel" was named in her honor.

When the Flamingo didn't turn a profit fast enough, the New York City Genovese crime family was not pleased. They suspected Bugsy was causing trouble with construction in order to rob his Mafia investors of millions of dollars. They also believed Bugsy was using Virginia to transfer money to Swiss bank accounts. While Virginia was on a trip to Paris, Bugsy was shot to death on June 20, 1947, in Virginia's Beverly Hills mansion. When police questioned her, she denied being his mistress or even that she was aware of his ties to the mob.

In 1951, Virginia was subpoenaed to testify before the Kefauver hearings and denied having any knowledge of organized crime. She told investigators that her income came from gifts from her boyfriends. The Internal Revenue Service determined that she had spent $500,000 without paying taxes and sued her. Virginia married well-known Sun Valley ski instructor Hans Hauser and moved with him to Europe. The IRS seized her house and property and auctioned them off for back taxes. The FBI placed her at number three on its Ten Most Wanted list.

Virginia, possibly one of the most famous female mobsters, spent her last years in Europe, separated from her husband and supported by their only child, Peter Hauser, who worked as a waiter. She died of an overdose of sleeping pills, an apparent

Virginia Hill, mistress of Bugsy Siegel.

Benjamin "Bugsy" Siegel.

suicide, near Salzburg, Austria, on March 24, 1966, at the age of forty-nine. Her body was found in a secluded area by a bridge crossing the Alterbach, a small stream. She is buried in Aigen Cemetery in Salzburg.

CHAPTER 18

FRED, THE TOWN DOG

Nobody knows where he came from, but a sick little puppy that showed up in Rockford, Alabama, in 1993 brought life back to the town that saved his.

When he first arrived, some folks in town were afraid he might spread a disease called "red mange." Turns out all the little guy had was a case of flea infestation. With his friendly disposition and natural love of people, he quickly became the town mascot. More than a mascot, really—Fred became a part of the town family.

The small, rural town of Rockford has just around four hundred residents. At the time Fred arrived, the town was struggling as businesses were closing and residents were leaving in search of better job opportunities. Fred helped spread a feeling of hope and put a smile on the faces of those who passed him on his daily rounds.

Fred didn't live the life of just any country dog. He spent most of his days at Ken's Package Store or roaming about town, and he spent his nights in a doghouse with "Fred the Town Dog" over the door. A "Fred Jar" collected spare change for his food.

For Halloween, Fred was known to appear dressed as a vampire. At Christmas, he wore his Santa hat, and then there were the bunny ears for Easter.

By 1998, Fred had his own column in the local paper, accompanied by a photo of the pup in his red bandana. Ghostwriters reported on town activities through the eyes of the dog. Eventually, news outlets around the state and farther began to take note. The British Broadcasting Corporation

Monument to Fred, the "Town Dog" in Rockford, Alabama, 2013. *Photo by Beverly Crider.*

(BBC) even dropped by for a visit. In 1999, Fred hit the big time when he appeared on the Animal Planet network.

Fred passed away in 2002, but Rockford residents still remember him with joy. He is buried behind the town's old jailhouse. A full-size tombstone, donated by a Montgomery businessman, was added in 2003. Fred was inducted into the Alabama Veterinary Medical Association Animal Hall of Fame in 2004.

PART II
LEGENDARY CREATIONS

CHAPTER 19

WINDSHIELD WIPERS

WHY DIDN'T I THINK OF THAT?

Imagine driving a car in the pouring rain, or even a heavy mist, and having no method for clearing your windshield. In the days of the "horseless carriage," you really didn't have many options. It, apparently, never occurred to the men who developed this new mode of transportation that there might be the need for some way to drive in inclement weather other than holding your head out the window as you drove. No, that took the ingenuity of a woman—an Alabama woman, to be more precise.

Mary Anderson (1866–1953) was born in Greene County. Mary's father died when she was four, but Mary and her sister, Fannie, and mother continued to live off the proceeds from his estate. In 1889, they moved to Birmingham and built the Fairmont Apartment building at 1211 Twenty-first Street South on the corner of Highland Avenue.

It was during a 1903 visit to New York City when Mary noticed drivers stopping every so often to manually scrape off their windshields. She saw others frantically rolling down their windows so they could stick their heads out the side windows to see. The only method available to moderate the effects of water on a windshield was to rub a plug of tobacco, a half onion or a piece of carrot briskly over wet windshields to promote visibility. Theoretically, they imparted an oily film to the glass, which prevented droplets from collecting, thereby helping you see where you were going. Mary knew there was a better way.

Upon returning to Alabama, Mary began to draw up plans for a device for cleaning a windshield that could be activated from inside the automobile.

Mary Anderson of Greene County was the first person to develop plans for a device for cleaning an automobile windshield that could be activated from inside the car. Her plans were very similar to modern windshield wipers. Her patent expired, however, as there was no interest in such a "frivolous" contraption in the very early days of automobiles.

Her plans were very similar to modern windshield wipers. She developed a plan for a swinging arm with a rubber blade. The device consisted of a lever that caused a spring-loaded arm to swing the blade across the windshield and back to its original position. The patent for Mary's windshield wiper (U.S. Patent #743,801) was issued in November 1903. Similar devices had been developed earlier, but Mary's was the first to prove functional. The device could be removed by the driver when clear weather returned.

Mary tried to sell her design but had no luck. In 1905, she contacted a Canadian firm, but the company saw no commercial value in the device and declined to produce it. She apparently did not continue the effort to market her invention and allowed her patent to expire.

At the time she applied for her patent, Henry Ford's Model A had not yet been manufactured, and he was years away from creating his famous Model T. Many people teased Mary for her frivolous invention. They didn't laugh long, however. By 1913, thousands of cars were on America's roads, and mechanical windshield wipers were standard equipment.

Anderson died on June 27, 1953, at the age of eighty-seven, while at her summer home in Monteagle, Tennessee. She was buried in Elmwood Cemetery in Birmingham. The *New York Times* and *Time* magazine carried her obituary for the sole reason that she invented the window-cleaning device for cars and other vehicles.

CHAPTER 20

JOHN PRATT

INVENTOR OF THE TYPEWRITER?

Long before the ease of spell check and autocorrect, writers were simply searching for an easy way of putting words on paper. Writer's cramp and bad penmanship can lead some frustrated authors to feats of ingenuity.

Attorney John Pratt of Centre, Alabama, was an investor in the newspaper the *National Democrat* and later served as editor of the *Gadsden Times*. Tired of bruised fingers from so much writing, he decided to create his own "writing machine" based on a printing wheel principle.

The eruption of the Civil War made it impossible for him to receive financing for his machine, known as the "pterotype." He moved to England and, in 1867, secured a patent for his machine there. A unique feature of the machine was that the typefaces were on a type plate, which was moved horizontally and vertically by the keys, and a hammer struck the paper from behind, driving it against the type. His invention created enough intrigue to be written about in *Scientific American*, but despite what many locals might want to believe, the Pratt pterotype was not the first typewriter invented. In fact, many inventors of the time were working on variations on the concept.

Some early attempts at typewriter design were intended to help blind people write. Pellegrino Turri built a working machine in 1808 for his blind friend countess Carolina Fantoni da Fivizzono. Between 1829 and 1870, there were many patents granted that never made it to production.

Still, Pratt, who some consider the "grandfather of the typewriter," should be given credit for helping inspire the man generally acknowledged as the inventor of the typewriter. Christopher Latham Sholes of Pennsylvania was

John Pratt's invention of an early typewriter known as the pterotype.

granted a patent in 1864 with his friend Samuel Soule for a page-numbering machine. A fellow inventor, Carolos Glidden, suggested that Sholes might want to consider incorporating letter printing into his machine. He referred Sholes to Pratt's pterotype.

It was 1870 before the first typewriter came into commercial production. It didn't look like what we consider a typewriter today (but then, today, how many kids even know what a "typewriter" looks like?). Malling Hansen's "writing ball" was a metal sphere with letter keys on it. The sphere moved until the right key came into contact with the paper.

Remington began production of its first typewriter, the Sholes & Glidden, in 1873, introducing the qwerty keyboard.

Sadly, Pratt's fame in the United States does not extend a great distance past his home county of Cherokee, although he is well known across England.

CHAPTER 21

THE ALABAMA INDESTRUCTIBLE DOLL

The "Alabama Baby," also known as the "Alabama Indestructible Doll," was born at the turn of the twentieth century. Her creator was Ella Gauntt Smith of Roanoke, who stumbled upon what would become one of the first female-owned businesses of the century.

One of Ella's young neighbors brought a broken bisque doll to her for repairs, as she was known as a skilled seamstress. Ella began repairs on the doll in 1899 and continued working on it for two years, trying various methods of repair. She finally came upon a method by which she poured the head full of plaster, covered it with a scrap of knitting and then repainted the features. After sewing the head onto the body, she replaced the wig.

Ella received the first patent on her doll in 1901 but had to use her husband's name, as women of the time could not be granted patents. In 1904, she won the blue ribbon for her dolls at the St. Louis Exposition at the World's Fair. Not only was her female-owned business making headlines for her "Alabama Baby," but she also was breaking new ground in the South by becoming the first doll maker to manufacture black dolls. Approximately 10 percent of her production (which reached around ten thousand dolls at its peak) was black.

As her business grew, Ella hired ten to twelve women to help with the work, instructing them in how to mold doll heads from a heavy fleece-lined fabric, as well as other tricks of the trade. She moved her work to an outbuilding that her husband built for her as a doll factory. There she worked in a locked room on the second floor with a hymn-singing parrot on her shoulder. Known

"A rare original Ella Smith Doll, with turned head and applied ears." *Photo for "Roanoke, Alabama: Home of the Ella Smith Doll," an Alabama Local Legacies project.*

for her love of animals, Ella used carrier pigeons for her business correspondence.

The "Alabama Baby," also known as the "Roanoke Doll," earned the name of the "Indestructible Doll" when, legend has it, a child dropped a doll in the street, where it was run over by a truck and remained undamaged.

Unfortunately, Ella's rise to fame took a turn for the worse in 1922. Two Roanoke businessmen wanted to share in her popular business and agreed to represent Ella's company, as partners, at the Toy Fair in New York. There, they received hundreds of orders for the dolls, all of which were lost when the men's train derailed near Atlanta, killing them both.

The men's grieving families accused Ella of causing their beloved family members' deaths and sued her for a sizeable amount. The tragedy of her loss compounded the effects of her diabetes and kidney disease. She died in April 1932.

CHAPTER 22

THE VAN DE GRAAFF GENERATOR

If you've ever visited a science museum, you've probably encountered a Van de Graaff generator—you know, that big ball that makes your hair stand on end and creates magnificent shows of "lightning." You might not realize that Robert Jemison Van de Graaff, for whom that device is named, was a Tuscaloosa native.

Robert's brothers were football heroes at the University of Alabama (UA). Hargrove Van de Graaff nearly lost an ear in a 1913 game against Tennessee. Apparently, his ear was cut so badly during the game that it was dangling from his head. Hargrove tried to rip it off so he could continue the game, but his teammates convinced him to get it bandaged. W.T. "Bully" Van de Graaff became Alabama's first All-American. Robert's third brother, Adrian, also played football for UA.

The youngest of the Van de Graaff brothers, Robert, also showed a talent for the game but suffered a broken femur and damaged his back during a Tuscaloosa High School football game. He spent most of his senior year recuperating in his family's mansion, built by his great-grandfather on Greensboro Avenue.

Robert earned a master's degree in mechanical engineering at the University of Alabama in 1923. He received a state grant in 1924 to study at the Sorbonne in Paris, where he attended lectures by radiation pioneer Marie Curie. The next year, he won a Rhodes Scholarship to study at Queen's College in Oxford, where Ernest Rutherford was experimenting with atomic particles.

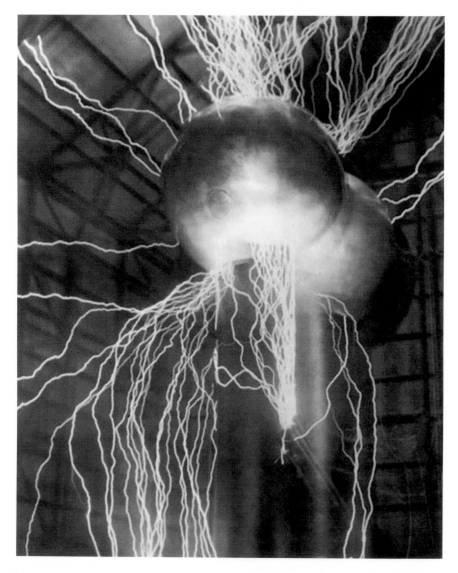

Van de Graaff generator. *Institute Archives and Special Collections, MIT Libraries, Cambridge, Massachusetts.*

Robert graduated from Oxford with a PhD in physics in 1928. He returned to the United States with the idea of a particle accelerator in 1929, when he joined the Palmer Physics Laboratory at Princeton University. There, he constructed a working model of an "electrostatic accelerator" capable of generating eighty thousand volts. By November 1931, his design was able to produce over one million volts. He demonstrated his device at the inaugural dinner of the American Institute of Physics. A patent for the Van de Graaff generator was awarded in February 1935.

Harvard Medical School was the first to use the generator clinically to produce X-rays for the treatment of cancerous tumors with radiation in 1937. Another use for the technology was in the development of the atomic bomb. Scientists who worked on the famous Manhattan Project used Robert's accelerator in developing the bomb that was dropped on Hiroshima.

In 1946, Robert started the High Voltage Engineering Corporation (HVEC), which soon became a major supplier of electrostatic generators used for cancer therapy, radiography and the study of nuclear structure in scientific laboratories. The beam-control techniques developed there made possible the manufacture of microchips by shooting atoms into silicon.

By the time he died in Boston on January 16, 1967, at the age of sixty-five, there were more than five hundred Van de Graaff particle accelerators in over thirty countries around the world. The International Astronomical Union designated a crater in the Sea of Ingenuity in Van de Graaff's honor, and he was inducted posthumously into the Alabama Engineering Hall of Fame in 1989.

CHAPTER 23

THE WORLD'S FIRST AIRPORT

Thanks to a magnificent young Eastaboga man in his flying machine, Alabama is home to what many believe to be the world's first airport. Dr. Lewis Archer Boswell, born on May 9, 1834, was a pioneer aviator who some believe made the first powered heavier-than-air flight, predating the Wright brothers by several years.

Technically, Boswell was a Virginia native, but he moved with his bride, Miss Bettie Liddell, to Red Hill, her family's Talladega County plantation, in 1869, so we'll claim him as our own. He had published articles on aeronautics and had built a toy-size flying machine prior to moving to Alabama. It was here, however, that he built a full-size version. According to witnesses, some of whom lived well into the twentieth century, he made several flights across his cotton fields, using a barn roof as a launching platform.

Boswell left behind no written flight logs or photographs, so there is no physical proof of his accomplishment. He did patent two important aeronautical inventions: a propeller wheel (1874) and a steering mechanism (1903). He also invented a tricycle-like undercarriage, the forerunner of the one still common on airplanes today. Some Talladega County residents claimed that the Wright brothers knew of Boswell's work and offered him $50,000 for his plans.

Shortly after the Civil War, during which he served as a Confederate army surgeon, Boswell read an article on bird flight written by the Duke of Argyle in the *Edinburgh Review*. It was then that he began to think that people could fly through the air, with proper adjustments, just like birds.

He began working on a model of a machine that would allow people to fly in 1868 but destroyed the finished product by throwing it into the Yazoo River. Nobody knows what prompted him to do such a thing, but it wasn't his last effort. Convinced he was on to something unique, he continued work on his invention after his marriage in 1869.

Boswell had a jeweler in Talladega build a second model airplane from his plans before he applied for a patent. This model was about twelve inches long and was propelled by a clock spring mechanism. It was capable of flying across the room. Mrs. Boswell and her sons recalled the demonstration years later. Mrs. Boswell referred to it as an "aerial boat."

Boswell submitted the "aerial boat" with the patent application in 1874. He didn't save copies of much of his correspondence, unfortunately. He apparently spent so much time on his invention that he let his medical practice slide. He was not able to pay the $1,000 it would cost to buy the equipment needed to make the motor for his airplane. He was turned down for bank loans.

According to an article in *Alabama Aviator*, one letter he wrote to the secretary of war in 1900 survived. In this correspondence, Boswell told the secretary, "You need a flying machine." In this letter, he asked for a $1,000 loan to get Duryea Power Company of Reading, Pennsylvania, to make a triple-cylinder gasoline engine for him. He promised to complete the airplane in sixty days and offered his Alabama property as collateral.

"I have contrived all needful devices to ascend and descend at will, with ease and safety, and to guide right and left as readily as one does a canoe on a still lake," he wrote. His offer was turned down.

On December 17, 1903, Orville and Wilbur Wright unveiled their flying machine at Kitty Hawk, North Carolina. At the time of Boswell's death in 1909, his pioneering achievements had been forgotten as the Wright brothers made worldwide headlines.

The former Talladega Municipal Airport, located on the land at one time owned by Dr. Boswell, has been renamed in his honor. Many believe what is now known as Boswell Field is "the world's first airport."

Boswell's plantation is now owned by the International Motorsports Hall of Fame, which has an exhibit devoted to his work and legend. He is buried in Oak Hill Cemetery west of Talladega. His tombstone mentions only his military service, but a historical marker at the site reads: "Invented a flying machine in the 1800s. Recorded witnesses stated that they saw it airborne."

CHAPTER 24

FOLK ART OF THE GODWIN BROTHERS

I caught my first glimpse of world-renowned folk artist Ronald Godwin as he peddled his small bicycle down the gravel road between his workshop and his home in Brundidge, Alabama. When I first saw him close up, my eye was immediately drawn to what I thought was a "walking boot" worn to support a broken ankle. When I looked more closely, I realized he was wearing one beat-up white tennis shoe and one ragged black shoe with the toe torn back, exposing his white sock–covered toes.

When I caught myself about to offer sympathies on his injury, he explained he was very superstitious and always wore one beat-up shoe for good luck. I have heard of many strange superstitions, so I just assumed this eccentric folk artist had one such superstition. Then I saw a twinkle in his eye, and he chuckled, "I have a corn, and this is more comfortable."

And that began my "by chance" meeting with the artist who sculpted the famous *Strider of Chernobyl* masterpiece.

Godwin created the metal sculpture of a bizarrely deformed fish in response to the Chernobyl nuclear reactor meltdown of 1986. Only one year after the disaster, he was working as a sculptor in New York City and decided to use his artwork to display his outrage over the catastrophe. He wanted to display the piece on a Manhattan sidewalk, but the city refused to allow it.

Not dissuaded at all, Godwin and some buddies managed to get the sculpture out on the sidewalk themselves. Godwin then called up a buddy at the *New York Post* and told him to get someone out there quickly to photograph the sculpture because he was about to be arrested.

Strider of Chernobyl by folk artist Ronald Goodwin, located in Brundidge, Alabama, 2012. *Photo by Beverly Crider.*

As it turned out, the sculpture was photographed by many prominent newspapers and television stations and welcomed by the public. The city decided to allow the sculpture to remain on display for a couple weeks. The *Strider* is now one of Godwin's showpieces in his "sculpture park" on North Main Street.

The Fukushima Daiichi nuclear disaster that occurred following the Tōhoku earthquake and tsunami prompted Godwin to again express his concern through his artwork. The *Scorpion from Fukushima* is now on display next to the Chernobyl-inspired piece.

Godwin says he gets visitors from around the world—some stumble upon his work, while others seek it out. He can't understand their languages but shows them through his workshop anyway.

This outdoor sculpture park is open 24/7 and is free to the public. Ronald's brother, Larry, owns Art Wurks, about three miles south of Brundidge on U.S. Highway 231, where you'll find more pieces of southern folk art. You probably have seen much of the brothers' work already, even if you didn't know it was theirs. The brothers' father, Bob Godwin, owned a feed mill that served hundreds of dealers in three states. Ronald and Larry were artists at heart and did not feel the call toward the family business. They decided they could contribute to their father's business by focusing on marketing his products through large sculptures.

Giant rooster made of car bumpers by folk artist Larry Godwin, located on U.S. Highway 231, three miles south of Brundidge, 2012. *Photo by Beverly Crider.*

Rusty the dog (or the Big Red Dog) in Northport, the Rooster made of Car Bumpers in Brundidge, the Monument to the Hog in Dothan and many more around the state have their stamp all over them.

CHAPTER 25

THE *STORYTELLER*

PAGAN SCULPTURE OR PLAYFUL STATUE?

The *Storyteller* fountain in the heart of Birmingham's Five Points South has stirred up quite a lot of controversy during its relatively short time in town. The sculpture, featuring a central figure with the head of a ram, is located in front of the Highlands United Methodist Church where Twentieth Street South, Eleventh Court South and Magnolia Avenue converge. It has become a popular local landmark.

Storyteller fountain at Five Points South in Birmingham, Alabama, 2012. *Photo by Beverly Crider.*

Storyteller fountain at Five Points South in Birmingham, Alabama, 2012. *Photo by Beverly Crider.*

The work was commissioned by the Birmingham Art Association from Alabama sculptor Frank Fleming in late 1985 and dedicated in late 1991. The *Storyteller* sits on a stump, reading to his animal friends from an open book, holding a staff topped with an owl (perhaps he has just received an owlgram from Hogwarts). His listeners sit on a circular platform, and a hare rides on the back of a tortoise. Five frogs spit water arcs crisscrossing the fountain.

Since its installation, the sculpture's central figure has been described by some as a satanic symbol. Some have gone so far as to say the frogs listening to the "ram-man" or "goat-guy" are arranged at the points of a satanic pentagram. Fleming has denied any such association and has stated that he intended the figure to convey a gentle, peaceful attitude. The homeless community around Five Points South has welcomed "Bob," as they call the figure, into its ranks and considers him a kindred spirit.

Fleming says he sculpted the animals out of old southern storytelling traditions employing fun creatures and, because he wanted the sculpture to interest children, conveying the idea of storytelling as a "peaceable kingdom."

CHAPTER 26

POPEYE, ALABAMA'S SAILOR MAN

B et you didn't know the character famous for saying, "I yam what I yam and that's all that I yam," worked the Coosa River in Alabam. Well, the man who was the inspiration for the character did, anyway.

"Fantastic as Popeye is, the whole story is based on facts," cartoonist Tom Sims told Hughes Reynolds in a 1944 interview for *The Coosa River Valley from De Soto to Hydroelectric Power*. "As a boy I was raised on the Coosa River. When I began writing the script for Popeye I put my characters back on the old *Leota* that I knew as a boy, transformed it into a ship and made the Coosa River a salty sea."

Tom's father was the captain of the *Leota*, formerly the steamboat *Annie M.*, which was built by the River Iron Company of Gadsden to push barges to the furnace. After it was purchased by the federal government and renamed *Leota*, the steamboat was used to help rebuild low-lift dams on the Coosa River.

Tom began drawing the comic strip *Thimble Theater* after the strip's creator, Elzie Segar, died in 1938. The storyline was centered on the Oyl family, who owned a shipping business. One of the sailors who worked for Commodore Oyl was a wise-cracking, spinach-eating chap who spun off into its own comic strip, *Popeye the Sailorman*. He and his wife lived in Ohatchee, Alabama, during most of the time Tom wrote the strip. Tom did all his work for King Features Syndicate by mail and never considered the strip a big deal.

Tom liked to use local Ohatchee residents in his strip, including a neighbor who tied a cow to a tree in his yard to be used as a "live lawn mower." Tom

As a boy, cartoonist Tom Sims was raised on the Coosa River. When he began writing the script for *Popeye*, he put his characters back on the old *Leota* that he knew as a boy, transformed it into a ship and made the Coosa River a salty sea.

Tom Sims, creator of the *Popeye the Sailorman* comic strip.

also spent a couple of years writing the *Blondie* comic strip, provided ideas for *Amos 'n' Andy* and wrote the script for the characters' motion picture, *The Big Broadcast*. He also wrote for the animated *Tom and Jerry* movie cartoons.

CHAPTER 27

FA-SO-LA SINGING

*There is melody in the very phrase, and the image it conjures—the church in
the grove, soaring harmonies, feasting and fellowship—has somehow remained
central to the South's idea of itself. It soothes the soul like a remnant of Eden,
or a preview of the Promised Land. In a culture increasingly immune to simple
pleasures, few Southerners today partake of such an experience by any means more
direct than secondhand nostalgia. There exists in our midst, however, a wellspring
of the living past.*
—*Sacred Harp Musical Heritage Association*

Since the early nineteenth century, congregations from Athens to Mobile
have nurtured and sustained what some folklorists have called one
of Alabama's most remarkable cultural jewels. Sacred Harp singing, the
largest surviving branch of traditional American shape-note singing, takes
its name from the songbook *The Sacred Harp*, first published in 1844. Also
known as "fa-so-la" singing, the a cappella musical style actually predates
the publication of the book.

Appalled at the lack of musical skills displayed by their congregations,
New England clergy of the eighteenth century developed singing classes
to teach their members ways to improve their vocal abilities. The classes
became so popular that the singing method soon spread into the surrounding
community and became an integral part of the area's social life.

New creative, lively pieces created by the locals did not conform to rigid
European conservatory rules of the times. The new songs were based on the

Scottish and English church music that made free use of counterpoint and dance rhythms coupled with loose harmonic rules. This may explain why some people today, hearing shape-note music for the first time, compare it to the bagpipe. Many of the tunes do employ a five-toned scale of ancient Celtic origin.

The New England singing schools fell out of favor shortly after the Revolutionary War when an influx of European trained musicians campaigned for the removal of this "crude and lewd" music. Were it not for two crucial events, this art form might have faded from existence.

The development of a four-shape notational system by Little and Smith in 1801 complemented the oral four-syllable system already in place in the singing schools, allowing the songs to be put down on paper. That, coupled with the spread of the music by itinerant singing schoolmasters into the South, gave shape-note singing a foothold. It was in the South where the marriage of the New England singing school music to the oral Celtic folk tune was completed, and the folk-hymn was born.

Sacred Harp singing combines the old European practice of solmization, or syllable singing, with various systems of "patent" notation. One of four shapes is assigned to each note of the seven-tone scale. Only four shapes are used because there are only four syllables sung for the seven primary notes of the scale. The right triangle was designated *fa*, the oval *sol*, the rectangle *la* and the diamond *mi*.

During the latter half of the nineteenth century, the development of gospel music overshadowed the old-fashioned four-shape folk-hymns. But in many regions of Tennessee, Georgia, Alabama, Mississippi and Texas, a tradition of singing conventions took shape in which people would sing for hours or days at a time. "Dinner on the Grounds" mixed socializing with singing, and young singers were given an opportunity to try out their new skills.

Rural southerners have preserved this musical heritage in a continuing oral tradition. While most shape-note books have died out, there is still a large singing tradition based on the Sacred Harp. Compiled in 1844, the book has never gone out of print and is available in several versions. Each new edition of the book preserves the music that has gone before and includes new compositions that are similar in form and style to the older pieces.

The success of the movie *Cold Mountain*, which featured Sacred Harp singings recorded in Henager, Alabama, sparked renewed interest in the tradition. Whether because of the success of the movie or any number of other reasons, new singers, especially outside the South, are "discovering" this style faster than ever before, according to Sacred Harp Musical Heritage Association. Newsletters keep singers informed of activities across the country, and the National Sacred Harp Convention draws hundreds of singers to Birmingham every June.

PART III
BELIEVE IT OR NOT

CHAPTER 28

LIGHTNING STRIKES MORE THAN TWICE

William Cosper of Childersburg was born in 1838, but it was his death in 1919 that landed him on a list of the one thousand strangest stories in the United States more than half a century later. William was struck by lightning while at home with his wife, Martha. After recovering from this near-death experience, he was struck again and was not so lucky the second time.

His family laid him to rest in the Childersburg Cemetery, where his headstone was also struck by lightning. The family replaced the destroyed marker with another headstone, which also was destroyed by lightning. The family could not afford a third marker, so his headstone lies in pieces to this day. Bricks and stones lie atop what was left of the grave marker.

Burial site of William Cosper in the Childersburg Cemetery. All that remains of the headstone is a pile of stones. 2013. *Photo by Beverly Crider.*

CHAPTER 29

THE WRIGHT BROTHERS MAKE FLIGHT HISTORY IN ALABAMA

J ust seven years after Orville and Wilbur Wright made the first sustained controlled powered airplane flight at Kitty Hawk, North Carolina, the brothers began searching southern cities for a location for a civilian flying school. The Wright brothers hoped to turn their invention into a profitable commercial venture by training instructor pilots to "teach buyers of the machines how to operate them."

After visiting several sites in Georgia and Florida, Wilbur Wright met with a group of Montgomery, Alabama businessmen. In exchange for locating a flying school in the Montgomery area, these businessmen offered Wright an old cotton plantation owned by Frank D. Kohn free of charge. Due northwest of Montgomery, this area consisted of cotton farms and a small village known as Douglasville. The offer also included construction of a hangar and transportation to and from Montgomery. Toward the end of February 1910, Wilbur decided to open one of the world's earliest flying schools at the site that would subsequently become Maxwell Air Force Base (AFB).

Like he had done at Kitty Hawk in 1903, Orville Wright recorded the first powered flight in Montgomery's history. The local press reported, "A strange new bird soared over the cotton fields to the west of Montgomery, on March 26, 1910. It was the graceful airplane of Orville Wright, guided by the hand of the pioneer of the skies himself."

Wright took his pusher biplane up twice that day for five minutes each, never exceeding an altitude of fifty feet or a speed of more than forty miles

The biplane pictured here was used by Orville Wright to train students at his civilian flying school, which opened near Montgomery in March 1910.

per hour. Although only a few people witnessed the initial flights, hundreds more came to watch the almost daily flying activities that followed. By April, some flights had lasted for more than thirty minutes and had reached heights exceeding two thousand feet.

The Wright brothers selected five students for training. They taught their students the principles of flying, including takeoffs, balancing, turns and landings. The first recorded heavier-than-air night flights in aviation history occurred at the Alabama field on May 25, 1910. One newspaper article noted that the Wright flyer was seen "glinting now and then in the moonlight."

Shortly thereafter, the Wrights and two of their students returned to Dayton, Ohio, but the three other students continued to fly at the field for a few more weeks until this brief but significant chapter in aviation history quickly came to an end. A May 27, 1910 telegram from the Wright brothers directed the closing of the school. On the following day, the biplane was disassembled, placed onto freight cars and sent to Indianapolis, Indiana.

CHAPTER 30

AMERICA'S FIRST GRAFFITI

S ome Floridians may claim that they are home to America's oldest city, St. Augustine. However, there is evidence to suggest that Alabama's own Childersburg is the oldest continuously occupied city in the nation. And not only can the city claim to be first in occupation, but it is also home to the nation's oldest recorded cave, which holds the proud distinction of being the first site of cave graffiti in America.

St. Augustine, in northeast Florida, was founded in 1565 as San Augustin by Spanish admiral Pedro Menéndez de Avilés. Childersburg, however, was visited by Hernando DeSoto and his Spanish expedition in AD 1540, beginning the recorded history of Alabama. This makes Childersburg, the city nearest Kymulga Cave, later renamed DeSoto Caverns, the oldest continuously occupied settlement in the United States, predating St. Augustine by twenty-five years.

The DeSoto expedition spent several weeks in what was then the capital of the Coosa Indians, just a few miles west of DeSoto Caverns. Their mission—to find gold and to establish the first Spanish colony in the New World—was unsuccessful. The Coosa micco (chief) welcomed DeSoto during a ceremony near the entrance to the caverns. The micco offered DeSoto territory in which to establish a colony, but DeSoto turned down the offer because he had found no gold. Instead, despite the micco's offer, he took slaves from among the Coosa people and raided their storage bins for food.

Did some of DeSoto's party remain behind in what is now Childersburg? If so, as some believe, that would, indeed, support the city's claim to being the oldest continuously occupied city in the nation.

As for the oldest graffiti, in the early 1700s, one of the most-used trails for trading was the Charleston-Chickasaw, which passed right by DeSoto Caverns. A well-known landowner and Indian trader from the South named I.W. Wright used this trail. While resting during a trip in 1723, he chiseled his name and the year in rock. This marker is now on display at DeSoto Caverns and is described as the oldest inscribed marker or "graffiti" to be found in any U.S. cave.

Decades later, after the Revolutionary War ended, Benjamin Hawkins was appointed the U.S. agent among the Creeks and general superintendent of all tribes south of the Ohio River. In December 1796, he visited Upper Creek territory and, in his report to President Washington, described the beauty of DeSoto Caverns. This report makes DeSoto Caverns the first officially recorded cave in the United States.

During Prohibition, DeSoto Caverns were once again making history as one of the area's speakeasies. Moonshine was plentiful and gambling available to all interested. The location became the site of so many fights and shootings that it became known as the "Bloody Bucket," and federal agents closed it down. The "Bloody Bucket" was not reopened after Prohibition was repealed.

CHAPTER 31

MEMORIAL TO AN ASSASSIN

Joseph Pinkney "Pink" Parker was a Troy police officer, teacher and Confederate veteran. He's most remembered, however, for his hatred of Abraham Lincoln. He financed what was possibly the only monument to the memory of an assassin that stood on American soil.

Parker was born in Coffee County in 1839. He had just completed his studies at Spring Hill Academy when the Civil War started, and he left for the front. Four years later, he returned to find his once well-stocked farm overgrown with weeds, his stock and his slaves gone and his sister angered by the treatment she had received from Northern soldiers.

No longer able to afford his property, Parker took a position as a "walker," keeping the railroad tracks repaired. He later became a schoolteacher, but the parents of his students were too poor to pay his salary. He eventually regained some of his finances and built a nice home in Troy.

Nevertheless, Parker's hatred of Lincoln grew from year to year. Just the mention of his name would send Parker into outbursts of profanity that shocked those within earshot. The pastor of the Baptist church tried unsuccessfully to get him to censor his commentary. Finally, the church removed him from its rolls for his profanity. Parker was said to have remarked to a friend, "It wasn't quite fair. I know all the deacons in that church, and any one of them can cuss better than I can."

Each year on the anniversary of Lincoln's death, Parker dressed in his finest clothes to celebrate. He would even wear a paper badge reading "Anniversary of the Death of Old Abe Lincoln." At first, townspeople thought of him

Joseph Pinkney "Pink" Parker, out of hatred for Abraham Lincoln, commissioned a monument to honor his assassin, John Wilkes Booth. The stone was later re-purposed to serve as Parker's own headstone.

as nothing more than a harmless eccentric. It was the South and not that long after the Civil War, after all. By 1906, he took his hatred too far when he commissioned a monument to the memory of John Wilkes Booth for his assassination of Abraham Lincoln. Apparently, he didn't let his neighbors in on this plan, and it didn't go over too well when the four-foot-high monument was installed in Parker's front yard with the inscription: "Erected by Pink Parker in honor of John Wilks [sic] Booth for killing Old Abe Lincoln."

In 1920, the Woman's League of Republican Voters of Alabama launched a nationwide petition drive to get the monument torn down, apparently unaware that a few years earlier, boys had knocked over the monument as a Halloween prank. According to a 1951 pamphlet by Stewart Winning McClelland, no one ever replaced it. Still, the national attention generated by the petition placed the story of the monument in front of editors across the country, and it became major news.

By 1921, letters were arriving from across the country demanding that the monument be removed. During all the controversy, Parker died. His sons had the monument re-carved to serve as Parker's headstone on his grave in Oakwood Cemetery on Knox Street in Troy.

National press reports at the time contained a number of errors, including that funds for the monument had been raised by an outpouring of community support, which wasn't true. They also claimed the monument stood on the town square, also untrue. An article in the *Brooklyn Eagle* published on June

5, 1921, even printed the wrong date of the monument's installation, stating it was erected in 1866. The article continued:

> *The sentiment that condoned the political murder of the most lovable man in history is a curious thing to study after the lapse of more than half a century. The whole South of today honors Lincoln's memory. There are no pilgrims to the grave of John Wilkes Booth or to his monument.*
>
> *Yet the temporary existence of the sentiment that led to the erection of this monument is not surprising. Booth's crime in Ford's Theater, April 14, 1865, was concededly not actuated by personal hate, or by any motive, save the hysterical passions of a hysterical, bad actor. And the long conspiracy trials by court-martial that followed the crime and Booth's death as a hunted fugitive on April 26, trials in which Jefferson Davis, the former President of the Confederacy, was at first named as a factor in the plot, and which in the judgment of some Northern lawyers as well as Southerners resulted in the "judicial murder" of Mrs. Surrat, were calculated to inspire a certain tolerance for what Booth had done, at least in certain sections of the Cotton States.*

On June 9, just four days after the *Brooklyn Eagle* article appeared, the editor of the *Troy Herald* wrote to the editor of that paper. Even the Troy editor's comments seem to conflict with other reports by claiming a storm blew over the monument shortly before Parker moved out of state. The new owner of the property, he wrote, never replaced the stone, and it now "lies flat with the inscription buried in the ground and is not noticeable from the street." He wrote:

> *We regret very much that this article appeared in your paper because of the fact that the true facts in the case were not given. However, this is not the first time our city has been given undue publicity regarding this monument. Several years ago the* St. Louis Post-Dispatch *gave a full page writeup of it.*
>
> *I will state the facts in the case for your information and trust you will see fit to clear up the matter as the people of our city do not appreciate the publicity we are getting out of this thing.*
>
> *The monument, a very small one, something similar to a small head-stone we have all seen in small cemeteries, bears the inscription "erected by Pink Parker in memory of John Wilkes Booth for the killing of old Abe Lincoln." The little stone was set up in the front yard of this old man, and we want it thoroughly understood that it was erected by Mr. Parker himself*

and paid for with his own money. He says himself that not one penny was contributed or solicited.

The people of this town did not approve of the erection of such a monument when it was set up some 15 years ago. It was seen by very few people, as the old man's home was not on a principal street, and the people of this city now really are glad that the monument no longer stands. We are making the facts known to you simply because we do not care for the publicity we are getting about this matter and now that we have stated the facts to you we believe you will be fair enough to the people of this section to so state the facts in your excellent paper.

The "facts" continued to be reported in a conflicting manner. An article in the July 17, 1921 issue of the *Washington Post* read, "By order of the town council a monument to John Wilkes Booth, assassin of Abraham Lincoln, which has stood for a number of years in the yard of Pink Parker, a resident of this place, has been removed and its owner instructed not to restore it to its former position. It now occupies an obscure place in his barn."

We know for sure that the monument existed, as there are photographs of it, and we know that Pink Parker commissioned it. That takes care of the "who" and the "what." The "when" and the "where" are a matter of dispute. Well, we do know it was in Troy, but just where in Troy was it located—before it ended up as Parker's tombstone in Oakwood Cemetery?

CHAPTER 32

THE CHILES/WHITTED UFO SIGHTING

"THE TRUTH IS OUT THERE!"

Like *The X-Files'* Fox Mulder, many of us, if the truth be known, do want to believe in life on other planets. One UFO case that has yet to be disproved occurred right here in Alabama.

The Chiles-Whitted sighting took place on July 24, 1948, over Montgomery. It was one of the very first reports of a large UFO officially filed by commercial airline pilots. Giving it credibility was that two career pilots, Captain Clarence S. Chiles and co-pilot John B. Whitted, made the report. The pilots were flying an Eastern Airlines DC-3 from Houston, Texas, to Atlanta, Georgia, at an altitude of five thousand feet when they encountered a giant cigar-shaped UFO that came very close to colliding with them.

It was 2:45 a.m. when a glowing object passed within one thousand feet on their starboard side, according to Chiles. Whitted estimated that the object was even closer. Both pilots agreed that it had no wings or tail section and that it had at least two rows of windows. They described the craft as having a pointed nose section and a "bluish glow" across the bottom from nose to end. An "orange-red" exhaust was emitted from the rear section. They estimated its length as being approximately that of a B-29 bomber.

The pilots reported the incident to Eastern officials and to Project Sign, the first major government UFO investigation project. They claimed they witnessed the object do an abrupt pull-up after the near-miss and Whitted observed it momentarily disappear after making a rapid vertical ascent. Their report further stated, "No disturbance was felt from airwaves, nor was there any wash or mechanical disturbance when the object passed."

Most passengers were asleep during the incident, but those who were awake agreed that something unusual happened in flight, although some differed in their account of what transpired. In the Naval Intelligence Report of the sighting, at least one passenger stated that the "DC-3 was rocked by the wash from the object." Some witnesses also described hearing a sound like that of a V-2 rocket.

Clarence McKelvie, who was assistant editor of the *American Education Press* at Columbus, Ohio, stated, "I saw no shape or form. It was on the right side of the plane, and suddenly I saw this strange, eerie streak out of my window. It was very intense, not like lightning or anything I had ever seen before."

Several witnesses at Robbins Air Base near Macon, Georgia, also reported seeing an object of the same description about a half hour before the DC-3 sighting. After poring through flight records of some 225 civilian and military flights from that morning, an official government investigation ruled out conventional aircraft as the object in question.

"What was that Thing that scared the daylights out of two Atlanta Eastern Air Line pilots in the spooky hours Saturday morning?" wrote William Key in the July 25, 1948 *Atlanta Journal*. "Is there some stratospheric Loch ness fire-breathing monster on the Milky Way run between Atlanta and New Orleans?"

Chiles and Whitted told the story of what they saw over Montgomery to the *Journal*:

> *A gigantic plane without wings, black against the night sky, streaking through the heavens at 5,000 feet altitude with a fiery comet's tail 25 to 50 feet in length. It had a 100 foot fuselage about four times the circumference of B-29s, and two rows of brilliantly lighted square windows. Creepiest of all, it was a veritable Flying Dutchman of the Skies. Nary a living soul was seen aboard!*

Project Sign eventually adopted the explanation that what the pilots and other witnesses observed was a meteor but added that the description of the object and its maneuvers did not match that of a meteor. This near-collision is still listed under the "unexplained" category. The Chiles-Whitted case file is considered to be one of the most significant in the early history of UFO research.

CHAPTER 33

HUEYTOWN HUM

For several months in 1992, a Birmingham suburb experienced a puzzling anomaly known as the "Hueytown Hum." The erratic, low-pitched noise kept people awake at night and set dogs to howling. The sound seemed to emanate from the hills surrounding Hueytown, located about fifteen miles southwest of Birmingham.

The hum would continue for up to three days at a time before fading, only to return within hours. The phenomenon even caught the eye of Ronald Smothers, a reporter for the *New York Times*.

"I catch myself trying to breathe in time with its rise and fall in pitch," a Hueytown woman told the reporter. "My dog Princess won't eat when it's going," she said.

A high school math teacher said it sounded like "the hum of a fluorescent light tube about to go."

The hum spawned numerous jokes and frivolous explanations. More serious speculators believed it was caused by electromagnetic forces and high-voltage power lines. The mystery was even more bizarre in that it seemed to affect only one area of town that included about five hundred homes.

The *Times* article quoted Clifford Bragdon, a professor of city planning at Georgia Institute of Technology, who said, "People try to get at these things by using the classical visual approach. But you need an acoustical Sherlock Holmes to solve things like this."

The hum also made its way into the papers in Nevada. Salt Lake City's *Desert News* reported that the noise was so loud that it disrupted some residents' prayers, while others didn't hear a thing.

Many residents began to put two and two together and came up with their own ideas when they took a closer look at the large ventilation fans that were installed in nearby coal mines. Timber had been cleared from a pine forest that had served as a buffer between Hueytown and the USX Corporations Oak Grove mines, ten miles west of Hueytown. Additionally, just south of USX's mines, Jim Walter Resources Inc. operated a mine with three fans, one of which operated at 3,500-horsepower with twelve-foot blades. The fan went into operation at about the time Hueytown residents recalled first hearing the hum.

CHAPTER 34

TALLADEGA JINX

Folklore surrounding what we now call the "Talladega Jinx" was active for centuries before the city known as Talladega even existed. Early settlers in the area known as Dry Valley spoke of "eerie forces," wrote Ed Hinton in a 2009 ESPN.com report. "The track itself was born under a bad sign in 1969, when the star drivers pulled out of the inaugural race due to the unknowns of the monstrous new track, the biggest and fastest ever built, 2.66 miles around with 33-degree banking."

In 1973, Bobby Isaac, one of NASCAR's early heroes, claimed he heard a voice inside his car tell him to stop and get out. Young newcomer Larry Smith died instantly when his car seemed to merely scrape against the track wall. There were a number of strange occurrences inside and outside the track over a period of decades.

But what caused this jinx, or curse, as some call it, in the first place? One legend claims a Native American tribe raced horses where the track was built. It was said that the tribe's chief was killed when thrown from his horse, thus starting the curse. Some believe the track was built on an Indian burial ground. Others say the Creek nation drove out another tribe for collaborating with Andrew Jackson, and their shaman cursed the land.

The jinx seemed to subside for a number of years and slipped to the background of track lore. Then came a race scheduled for Halloween 2009. With fear of the curse returning, track president Rick Humphrey invited Creek medicine man Robert Thrower to perform a traditional Native American balancing ceremony before race weekend. Thrower performed the ceremony on the start-finish line of the racetrack, asking specifically for balance to be restored to the land.

Several years ago, Dale Earnhardt Jr. was asked about the jinx and about the incident with Bobby Isaac in particular. According to a 2009 report on RacinToday.com, he answered, "You know, I believe it. Bobby Isaac comes in with the lead with 10 to go and tells you he heard a voice? You have to believe it...I definitely have a lot of respect for the racetrack. If what they say is true, you know, it would be kind of freaky."

CHAPTER 35

CHURCH WINDOWS BURIED IN GERMANY DURING WORLD WAR I

Among the prominent features of Cullman's Sacred Heart Catholic Church are the stained-glass windows, designed by the Von Gerichter Ecclesiastic Studio of Columbus, Ohio, in 1914. Twenty-four of the windows were built in Munich, Germany, but World War I broke out before the windows could be shipped to Cullman. The windows were buried in Germany to protect them. After the war, the windows were dug up and shipped to Cullman, where they finally were installed in 1920.

Father James Meurer, a German-speaking priest, founded the Sacred Heart parish in 1877. The first church was made of wood and served the parish for thirty-six years. The present stone church was dedicated in 1916, and the matching stone school was built in the years following World War II.

Sacred Heart's most prominent feature, the gold crosses atop its steeples, were part of a major restoration project conducted on the church steeples and roof in 1999. Those crosses, along with the stained-glass windows, survived another catastrophic event in 2011 when a massive tornado ripped through Cullman. Much of the city was destroyed, but the Sacred Heart Catholic Church remained standing with windows intact.

Sacred Heart Catholic Church in Cullman, Alabama, 2012. *Photo by Beverly Crider.*

CHAPTER 36

SWASTIKAS ON THE JEFFERSON COUNTY COURTHOUSE

S wastikas are etched on the Jefferson County Courthouse. Some of you may be surprised to learn this; others may have known for years. So, let's address the elephant in the room, so to speak: why?

Actually, the swastika is one of the oldest and most universal symbols around. It was long used by cultures around the world as a symbol of long life and good luck. It remains widely used in Indian religions, specifically in Hinduism, Buddhism and Jainism.

Western use of the symbol became subverted after it was adopted as the emblem of the Nazi Party. Since World War II, most Americans have known the swastika only as a Nazi symbol, which has led to confusion about its religious and historical status in other cultures.

The Jefferson County Courthouse, which is on the National Register of Historic Places, was built in Birmingham in 1931 by the Chicago firm Holabird and Root, which also designed Chicago's Soldier Field football stadium. Plans for the building were drawn up in the late 1920s. Many older buildings, built before the swastika became associated with Nazism, have swastikas built into their architectural decorations.

The original Penobscot Building in Detroit, Michigan, is one example. Built not long after the turn of the twentieth century, it was named for the Penobscot Indian tribe and region of Maine, the boyhood home of one of the investors. The Indian-themed detail of the building includes the use of the swastika, a symbol important to the Penobscots long before it was adopted by the Nazi Party.

Swastika on the columns of the Jefferson County Courthouse in Birmingham, Alabama, 2012. *Photo by Beverly Crider.*

The DeKalb County Courthouse in Sycamore, Illinois, is another. Built in 1905, it includes swastika-decorated railings. It was added to the National Register of Historic Places in 1978. The Garfield Monument in Cleveland, Ohio, dedicated in 1890 as a tomb and memorial for President James A. Garfield, contains swastika tile patterns throughout the floor. The building was added to the National Register of Historic Places in 1973.

Because the swastika was a popular symbol with the Navajo people, the Arizona Department of Transportation marked its state highways with signs featuring a right-facing swastika superimposed on an arrowhead. In 1942, after the United States entered World War II, the department replaced the signs.

These are just a few of the numerous examples around the country of the pre–World War II use of the swastika. So, to those who might question the reason for its use on a Birmingham building, the answer would have nothing to do with Hitler or his Nazi Party. As with so many other buildings, it was most likely just a common architectural symbol of its day or maybe an expression of hope for Birmingham's prosperity in the future.

PART IV

MYTHICAL CREATURES

Chapter 37

HOOP SNAKES AND RIVER MONSTERS

Sightings of hoop snakes have been reported since colonial times in North America. This snake grasps its tail in its mouth and rolls after its prey, thereby achieving great speed, especially when going downhill. At the tip of its tail is a highly venomous stinger. The snake straightens out at the last second, skewering its victim with its venomous tail. The only escape is to hide behind a tree, which receives the deadly blow instead and promptly dies from the poison.

Well, that's how the story goes, at least. But do "hoop snakes" really exist? There are some people who will swear they have seen one, even though no evidence exists to support the claim.

The hoop snake myth is one of the most persistent in the United States and even appeared in Pecos Bill stories. If you should encounter a hoop snake in the wild, legend has it, the best defense is to run as fast as you can and hope to find a fence to leap over. The hoop snake will have to uncoil to get through the fence, thereby slowing it down. Some have reported that diving through the hoop of the snake will cause it to run away.

One version has it that the hoop snake is inflated and that it is luminous at night. Another version says the reptile squirts a venomous fluid from its tail.

One likely origin to the hoop snake myth is the mud snake found throughout the coastal plain. The mud snake is very docile and refuses to bite, but its habit of pressing the spine-like tip of its tail against a captor's skin gives rise to the misconception that it can sting. It has, therefore, been given the nicknames "horned snake" and "stinging snake." Southern folklore also

A hoop snake chasing a young boy.

holds that the mud snake can take its tail in its mouth and roll like a wheel, giving rise to the common name "hoop snake." The snake is not capable of moving in this manner, however.

Adding to the mythic qualities of the mud snake, it is nocturnal and secretive, and its habitats are generally not frequented by humans. These snakes, therefore, are rarely encountered. Secretive creatures always make good fodder for creepy tales.

Of course, snakes were not the only creatures you had to be mindful of. There was a giant river creature known as "catzilla" to add to your list of monsters to beware of. "Catzilla" was said to be a species of catfish that reportedly grew to the size of Volkswagen Beetles at several dams along the Tennessee River.

In 1877, reports appeared in the *Gadsden Times* of sightings of serpents in the Coosa River. A fisherman near Ball Play Creek reported seeing a strange occurrence on the opposite bank. He went to investigate and said he came face to face with a twenty-foot-long creature with large fins before it slipped beneath the surface.

Sightings of this creature were reported for several years from Rome, Georgia, to areas near Gadsden. Each sighting included reports of a monster said to be fifteen to twenty feet long and covered with large fins. The creature always dipped beneath the water when anyone approached.

Eventually, a group of people picnicking at Ten Island near Ohatchee said they put an end to the monster when they spotted it. They claimed to have stoned it to death.

Other sightings of strange creatures have been reported by riverboat captains and workers constructing the first bridges and dams in and around the Coosa River in Etowah County. Divers who worked on the Neely-Henry Dam at Ohatchee reported sightings of giant catfish as large as a man.

Perhaps even stranger than the giant catfish sightings were reports of prehistoric-looking fish seen along the Coosa River known as alligator gar. The fish was said to resemble a saltwater barracuda, with a mouthful of razor-sharp teeth that reached several feet in length.

Chapter 38

SKUNK APE AND ALABAMA BOOGER

Skunk Ape

The so-called skunk ape is a malodorous monster that is considered a cryptid, or a creature whose existence has been suggested but is not recognized by scientific consensus. According to the folks over at SkunkApe.com, "The skunk ape supposedly hides in muddy, abandoned caves which is thought to create the awful 'skunk like' smell. Reportedly, these 'Skunk Apes' live in swamps, caves, forests, open grasslands, and at the edge of your backyard."

A "skunk ape spotter" in Alabama who goes by the name Ruby B. reported the following sighting on SkunkApe.com:

Well, I was going along and smelled something bad. I thought something had died and was stinking. Like maybe it was a cow or opossum or something.

Right after that I got into a big mess of cattails. I got kind of tangled up in them and it was wet and spidery and I got freaked so I pushed a bunch of those cattails out of the way and right in front of me was that beast. He was bigger than my husband, had hair all over, kind of red eyes, and really stunk to high heaven. I guess I scared him as bad as he scared me. We both turned around and hightailed it out of those marshes and that's the last I ever seen of him. I told my husband. He broke out his 3030 and went back there. He said he saw where we had been, but couldn't find hide nor hair of the beast. I know I didn't believe you a year ago, but I believe you now.

ALABAMA BOOGER

Then, there's the "Alabama Booger," a tall, black-eyed, hairy giant that terrorized folks in Chilton County, most notably around the Clanton area. Locals described it as tall, broad-shouldered, hairy from head to toe and downright frightening, according to the Big Foot Encounters website, which says, "Booger's a term related to 'boogey man stories,'—a scary man thing or campfire apparition usually associated with hairy giant specters or mysterious monsters."

CHAPTER 39

CHOCCOLOCCO MONSTER

If you watch *The Daily Show* with Jon Stewart on Comedy Central, you might be familiar with a little celebrity known as the "Choccolocco Monster" in Calhoun County. In May 1969, spooked drivers started reporting a monster in the woods between Choccolocco and Iron City on a road known as the Iron City Cutoff.

"As headlights approached, the awful thing would rear up on its hind legs and threaten to jump into the road," wrote Andy Duncan in *Alabama Curiosities*. "At least eight people reported seeing the thing. They agreed it had big teeth, a huge head, and a shaggy pelt and was about the size of a cow."

Normally, officials would scoff at the idea, but the United States was in the midst of Bigfoot Fever at the time, and hairy monsters in the woods made headlines. Locals and out-of-towners began cruising the back roads hoping to get a glimpse, or even capture, the Bigfoot wannabe.

When nobody ever successfully captured the monster, interest began to die off. More than thirty years later, on Halloween 2001, Neal Williamson confessed to the *Anniston Star* that he had been the Choccolocco Monster. A bored fifteen-year-old at the time, Williamson hotwired his parents' car and drove out to the lonely road. He wore a bedsheet and a long black coat and placed a cow skull over his head. Dancing by the side of the road, the "monster" had quite a time spooking drivers as they passed. That is, until one driver pulled out a rifle and fired at him. The Choccolocco Monster was seen no more.

Williamson revealed his identity to the world on Comedy Central's *The Daily Show*. You can watch the clip at http://www.thedailyshow.com/watch/mon-december-10-2001/ghosts-near-mississippi.

CHAPTER 40

WAMPUS CAT

The Wampus Cat is often compared to the Ewah of Cherokee mythology, who was a woman disguised in the skin of a cougar to spy on the men of the tribe. When the woman was discovered, the tribe's medicine man punished her by transforming her into a half-woman, half-cat.

This beast supposedly still roams the forest of Alabama and other areas of the Southeast. In some sections of rural East Tennessee, the Wampus Cat is

Sketch of one example of a wampus cat.

said to be the spirit of death and the earth. When her cry is heard, someone will die and be buried within the next three days.

According to one Alabama legend, the Wampus Cat was created as part of a governmental program in the 1940s and is believed to have been crossbred from a panther and a wolf. According to *Legends, Lore and True Tales of the Chattahoochee*, by Michelle Smith, "The U.S. government was thought to have created the animals to be used as messenger animals during World War II, much like pigeons were used in World War I. Something went wrong, and several of the hybrids escaped and bred in the wild. It is now believed that their offspring, the wampus cat, has populated all over Alabama and has even been seen as far north as the Appalachians."

The Wampus Cat got its name from the terms "catawampus" or "cattywampus," both old terms used to refer to "things that just aren't right," according to *Monsters of West Virginia* by Rosemary Guiley. "If you meet up with a Wampus Cat, bad luck and misfortune will strike. At the very least, you will go mad. The Wampus Cat is said to attack, maul, and kill farm animals, especially chickens, and to even attack humans."

CHAPTER 41

ALABAMA "WHITE THANG"

The Alabama "White Thang" has been known since the 1940s in the areas around Morgan, Etowah and Jefferson Counties, where people reported seeing a creature more than seven feet tall and covered in white hair. Reported sightings have come from Happy Hollow, Walnut Grove, Moody's Chapel and Wheeler Wildlife Refuge.

The creature is known for its ability to move quickly and produce an eerie screech that sounds like a woman's scream. Some have described the scream as sounding like that of a panther. Could the White Thang be an albino Bigfoot, another shy resident of the Alabama woods?

Peter J. Gossett of Winston County's FreeStateofWinston.org website writes that his aunt, Feneda Martin Smith, knew people who claimed to have seen the monster. Smith related her account on his website:

Old man George Norris...seen it over there in Enon graveyard, and he said it looked like a lion...you know, bushy, betwixt a dog and a lion. It was white and slick with long hair. It had a slick tail, down on the end of the tail a big ol' bush of hair. He lent up against a tree and fell asleep. When he woke up the sun was just rising, and the "white thang" was laying right beside him, and it was looking at him. He said it didn't offer to hurt him or nothing.

CHAPTER 42

BIGFOOT AND BLACK PANTHERS

BIGFOOT

Jim Smith of the Alabama Bigfoot Society says Tallapoosa County is among the hotspots in the state for Bigfoot sightings. However, he also receives many reports of sightings in areas that include Lee, Chilton, Blount and Cleburne Counties.

Smith told *Alabama Outdoors Magazine* of a possible way to "lure in" Bigfoot that he discovered by accident. He's hesitant to give out the information because he doesn't want anyone to use that knowledge to harm one.

A friend and I stumbled across a way to get close to the creatures, we think. We were conducting a Native American healing ceremony, or ritual you could call it, on myself. We had performed the ceremony on two or three different nights at the same location not looking for Bigfoot. Our only attention at the time was the healing ceremony. The place we were is thought to be a Power Place in Native American lore. Then, on the third or fourth night, we did see a Bigfoot reasonably close. Afterwards it seemed every time we performed this one ceremony, we would hear them close by, smell them or see one. We never felt threatened, but there have been times they got a little too close for my comfort.

"Bigfoot's shoes" on display at the Alabama Museum of Wonder in Seale, Alabama, 2012. Folk artist Butch Anthony used this pair of shoes to play a prank on the locals by leaving fake tracks in the woods. *Photo by Beverly Crider.*

BLACK PANTHERS

It is generally agreed by scientists that the last confirmed mountain lion in Alabama was killed around 1948 in St. Clair County. Free-ranging mountain lions can still occasionally enter the state, but these instances are not common.

Mountain lions range from northern Canada and Alaska to the southern tip of Chile. They are generally gray, red or brown in color. "Even though popular lore suggests they are black, there has never been a documented case of a black mountain lion in all of North America," according to wildlife biologist Frank Allen of the Alabama Division of Wildlife and Freshwater Fisheries. "There are only two species of large cats in the world that are known to be black," he wrote on OutdoorAlabama. com. "The leopard, which is found in Africa and Asia, in some cases, may be black. Another large cat that is rarely black in color is the jaguar, which lives from South America to Mexico and small sections of the southwestern United States. Other names for the mountain lion are puma, catamount, cougar and panther."

The nearest self-sustaining known wild population of mountain lions, called the Florida panther, is found in southwest Florida. They reside in the second-largest uninhabited block of land east of the Mississippi River. Since 1972, there have been forty-four panther/vehicle collisions confirmed in all of Florida. In Alabama, no mountain lion/vehicle collisions have been confirmed for at least sixty years, and there is no self-sustaining population of mountain lions currently known in Alabama. Resident populations appear to have been extirpated from Alabama in the mid-1800s.

Allen suggests that reports of mountain lion sightings in Alabama, although common, are probably cases of mistaken identity or released captives. "There have not been any confirmed reports by trail cameras, road kills, traditional photography, or hunter-harvested specimens since 1948. At last count there were around 30 game breeders who still retained permits to have captive mountain lions. New permits are no longer issued."

PART V
LEGENDARY PLACES

CHAPTER 43

BAMBOO FOREST

Tucked away in a twenty-six-acre park in Prattville is a bamboo forest used by the U.S. military for Vietnam-era combat training. The forest provided a humid environment with vegetation more similar to that found in Southeast Asia than most training sites on this continent.

"Wilderness Park," dedicated in 1982, was the first park of its type developed inside city limits in the United States. Areas of the forest have sixty-foot-tall bamboo with trunks six inches in diameter. Hundreds of varieties of plants are found there, including one of Alabama's largest beech trees.

The Park Information Board describes the history of the bamboo forest:

The area now designated a wilderness park was part of a land grant in 1823 to Joseph May, shortly after Alabama statehood. It was sold in 1835 to Daniel Pratt, the founder of the City of Prattville and over the next century passed to various owners. In 1940 the land was passed to Floyd Smith and he is the owner who placed the bamboo plants in the area. He had a love of exotic plants and acquired the bamboo shoots from a Washington Import firm. The small packet of plants were shipped through the mail and from that small beginning has grown the wonderful bamboo forest you see today.

CHAPTER 44

HAUNTINGS AT THE ST. JAMES HOTEL

The St. James Hotel in Selma is considered to be one of the most haunted places in Alabama. Many visitors to the hotel have reported accounts of hauntings and paranormal events. Located in the center of the historic district, overlooking the famous Alabama River, the building was constructed in 1837 and opened as the Brantley.

During the Civil War, the Brantley was occupied by Union troops during the Battle of Selma. Due to its concentration of Confederate arsenals and factories, the occupying army burned much of the city. Fortunately, the St. James and other structures on Water Street were spared. Together, they form the heart of the revitalized historic district and represent one of the finest collections of antebellum industrial buildings in the South. Following the war, the hotel was operated by Benjamin Sterling Turner, the first African American ever elected to the United States Congress. He reportedly hosted the legendary outlaw brothers Frank and Jesse James in 1881. In 1892, the hotel fell on hard times and ceased operations.

The doors were closed on the building and were not reopened for a century. A group of investors purchased the old hotel, and after putting in approximately $6 million in restorations, they were able to officially reopen the doors of the establishment in 1997 as the St. James Hotel.

Since its reopening, two of the most reported "hauntings" in the hotel include Jesse James and his girlfriend Lucinda. Several have claimed to have seen the apparition of a man dressed in attire that was common for a man in the late 1800s. He is most often seen in the rooms in which James typically

Right: Outlaw Jesse James.

Below: St. James Hotel in Selma, Alabama, 2012. *Photo by Beverly Crider.*

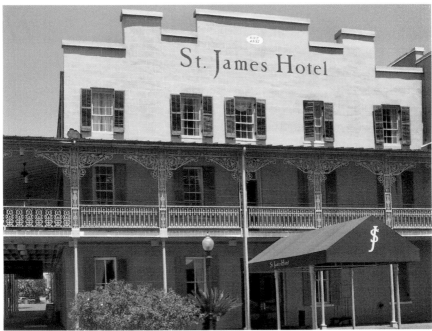

stayed: rooms 214, 314 and 315. However, the apparition has also been sighted at a certain table in the bar.

Many things are known about Lucinda. For one, she enjoyed the scent of lavender so much that when someone smelled the scent, they knew she was near. Today, several witnesses claim they are able to smell lavender with no logical explanation. In other instances, a full apparition of Lucinda is said to be seen walking the halls of the structure.

In the area of the courtyard, many strange events have been reported. First, several witnesses have observed what appears to be residual hauntings of individuals who are fully clothed in dress that was common to the 1800s. They seem unaware of the "living" surrounding them. Additionally, the sounds of apparent ghost dogs can be heard in the area. Jesse James, some have said, once owned a black dog that was his companion for many years. Many guests at the St. James have reported hearing a dog running up and down the halls. Also, guests in the hotel would often complain about a dog that would bark nonstop in the courtyard. When management would look into these complaints, no dog was ever found in the courtyard.

Whether you believe in the supernatural or just enjoy visiting beautiful historical landmarks, the St. James Hotel should be added to your list of must-see Alabama locations.

CHAPTER 45

GHOSTS OF THE GAINES RIDGE DINNER CLUB

Whether you're a history buff, ghost hunter or food connoisseur, there's one place in Camden, Alabama, that has it all. Gaines Ridge Dinner Club, located on Highway 10 E, is listed on the Alabama Ghost Trail and is owned by a member of the family for whom Fort Gaines in Mobile Bay is named.

The dinner club is located in an antebellum home built in the late 1820s. It once was the only two-story building between Black's Bluff and Allenton, two early settlements almost fifty miles apart. One of the early owners, Reverend Ebeneezer Hearn, a Methodist circuit rider, gave Gaines Ridge its historical name, "the Hearn Place." In 1898, the home passed into the family of its present owner, Betty Gaines Kennedy, who opened the restaurant with her sister Haden Gaines Marsh in 1985.

Like many old homes, Gaines Ridge has its share of ghosts. One of the most prominent is the lady who screams and calls out. "Miss Betty" tells the story of a particular night when she and one employee were working late. Betty went upstairs when she heard someone screaming for her. She ran down to the kitchen where the cook was working only to find the woman staring back at her. "Miss Betty, that wasn't me that called you," she said.

Another night, during business hours, Betty's daughter heard what sounded like someone falling in the ladies' restroom. She and guests at the restaurant heard a noise and saw the door shake. They were unable to open the door and assumed someone had fallen against it. When Betty arrived at the door, she also was unable to enter, and there was no response from inside

Gaines Ridge Dinner Club in Camden, Alabama, 2012. *Photo by Beverly Crider.*

the restroom. Finally, after Betty put some force into her shoving, the door opened only to reveal nobody inside the room.

As someone who loves history and loves a good ghost story, I, of course, had to check out this piece of southern folklore. After checking out the "haunted" locations around the home and enjoying a wonderful dinner, I left with beautiful memories but no ghost sightings. Within about a year, however, I was able to add a family ghost story of my own to the Gaines Ridge Legend.

My niece, Amy Davis, who is loath to visit anything resembling a haunted house, was persuaded by her mom to take a trip to Gaines Ridge for a nice family dinner. Her mom conveniently left out the tale of reported hauntings when describing the location to her, of course.

Amy; her husband, Matt; and their two small daughters joined her mom and dad for what she thought would be a nice dinner at a quaint historical location. As they were making their way from the car to the front door, Mia, her youngest, who was just beginning to talk, starting waving to the air and saying, "Hi, doggy!" She kept waving and speaking to what seemed to be a nonexistent animal. All kids are imaginative, right?

They now had reached the front porch just outside the front door to Gaines Ridge. At this point, Mia began to wave and speak to a little boy. Amy, who was becoming a bit uneasy at this point, asked Mia who she was speaking to and whether the little boy was inside or outside. Mia, who had a very limited vocabulary at this point, pointed to the window beside the front door and indicated "that" little boy, unable to understand why her mother could not see him.

Amy soon learned the legend of Gaines Ridge and asked that they be seated in any room other than the one currently occupied by a little boy apparently visible only to other very small children.

If you are more interested in history than in ghost stories, you might recognize the name of the establishment, as it is named for the same Gaines family as that of George Strother Gaines and his brother General Edmund Pendleton Gaines, who captured Aaron Burr and McIntosh Bluffs and for whom Fort Gaines in Mobile Bay is named. The antebellum mansion Gaineswood in Demopolis was also named in honor of the brothers.

CHAPTER 46

THE GOLLY HOLE

In December 1972, Shelby County, Alabama, became home to one of the largest sinkholes in U.S. history, aptly known as the "Golly Hole" by some and the "December Giant" by others.

Residents reported what sounded like a tremendous roar as the earth opened up, swallowing trees. Hunters in the area later discovered a sinkhole more than 300 feet wide (about the size of a football field) and between 120 and 150 feet deep.

The "Golly
Hole" of
Shelby County.

"Alabama does have a number of sinkholes across the state," said Sandy Ebersole with the Geological Survey of Alabama. "Primarily, they are located in north Alabama and south Alabama. Northern Alabama has a lot of soft limestone, which is responsible for a lot of sinkhole formation."

Alabama has more miles of underground rivers than any other state. Those rivers, known as groundwater, are responsible for most sinkholes. It moves through cracks and crevices in the area limestone, forming caves or caverns underground, according to the Geological Survey of Alabama. Eventually, the weight above those caves or caverns gets so heavy that the roof of the cave collapses, forming a sinkhole.

The "December Giant" apparently was dubbed the "Golly Hole" when friends of the property owners came back from their walk of the land and said, "You got a big hole on your property!" They walked up to the hole and said, "Golly!"

CHAPTER 47

BEAR CREEK SWAMP

The legend of Bear Creek Swamp, located just down the road from Prattville in Autaugaville, dates back generations. Locals claim if you drive through the area after dark, you're likely to spot phantom cars that fade into nothingness, floating orbs of light or even an upright creature that suddenly appears in front of your vehicle. There also is the tale of the ghost of a mother looking for her lost child in the swamp. Legend has it, if you repeat the phrase, "We have your baby" three times, she will attack.

Southern Paranormal Researchers, founded by Shawn Sellers of Montgomery, visited Bear Creek Swamp on the group's inaugural investigation. The dirt road that cuts through the swamp also winds its way through a couple miles of lonely woods and fields.

Sellers described the area in a report on wsfa.com:

> *The swamp used to be huge and the surrounding area was a virtual jungle. There is also an artesian well in the swamp. People still go there today and collect water that many believe holds magical powers. Every time I am there I drink some of the water. I figure that as much as I deal with the spiritual world, I need all the magic I can get. The swamp is not as big as it once was but when you are there you can feel the energy of what used to be there. There was a Creek Indian village on the land until 1814 and a lot of the settlers that settled that area were veterans of the Creek Indian War. The Creeks used the artesian water as healing water.*

During repeated visits to the swamp, the paranormal investigators say they have witnessed a number of unusual occurrences, including balls of light that they did not dismiss as swamp gas due to the behavior of the light. Sellers told the WSFA reporter:

> *There was one particular night that a ball of light crossed the road and turned. Shortly after, we heard what sounded like two hard knocks on the back of the truck. One night we had some cameras set up near the well and were walking down the dark swamp road.*
>
> *Suddenly, we saw two cars' headlights coming from opposite directions. As we backed off as far as we could to the side of the road, one of the cars raced past us suddenly going far faster than it should on such a road. We were afraid that there would soon be a collision. As we looked towards the other car, it slowly went past us in the opposite direction. To our amazement there was no collision or even a beeped horn. There was no place for the speeding car to go except into the swamps. We raced back to the well where we had our camera facing the road. We rewound the tape to see where the other car went and found no sign of the speeding car, only the slow car from the other direction.*

The swamp also attracted the attention of producers of the SyFy Channel's *Deep South Paranormal* show. A team visited the location for an episode of the first season in 2013.

HOUSE OF CROSSES

The late W.C. Rice's "Cross Garden" or "House of Crosses" in Prattville has experienced the effects of time but was still named one of *Time* magazine's Top 50 American Roadside Attractions as recently as 2010. "While frightening in its fervor, the collection is an example of folk art at its most primitive," wrote *Time's* Gilbert Cruz.

Roadside America also considered the site noteworthy. A team of writers got to talk with the man himself not long before his death in 2004.

"Rice put up his first crosses in 1976, after his mother died, inspired, he

W.C. Rice Cross Garden in Prattville, Alabama, 2012. *Photo by Beverly Crider.*

says, by a crossed wreath at her funeral. 'Down in the front there's three crosses and four pine trees. I believe in God, Jesus and the Holy Ghost... Pentecost, that's what we are. What I've done is what they told me to do. You know, they told Noah to build the Ark and he saved all those families, so I built it like they told me so I can save all MY families.'"

The many wooden crosses scattered around the property have become weathered, and the old household appliances with hand-painted Bible verses and warnings against sex and drugs are rusted and disintegrating. What once was a "must-see" destination is crumbling to the ground. The family originally planned to

W.C. Rice Cross Garden in Prattville, Alabama, 2012. *Photo by Beverly Crider.*

maintain the garden, and possibly add to it, after Rice's death. It appears the task may have been more than they anticipated. Still, it is quite a site to behold.

You can visit what's left of the Cross Garden in Prattville. It's located northwest of town on Highway 82 past the country club, over the hill and left on County Road 86.

CHAPTER 49

CRAGFORD'S HANGING TREE

A case of mistaken identity led to the murder of Mrs. Lobina Knight Mitchell in 1881 in the town of Wesobulga (now Cragford) in Clay County. Apparently, a man identified as Charles Jesse Waldrop was hired by Wesobulga resident Hal Mitchell to kill his wife. Living nearby was a man named Al Mitchell (no relation). Waldrop mistakenly killed Al's wife.

The *Carroll County Times* in Georgia reprinted the account given to Alabama's *Randolph County News* in its July 8, 1881 issue:

> *About 8 o'clock Wednesday morning, Mrs. Mitchell, wife of Mr. Al Mitchell, left home to visit a relative a short distance off and when about a half a mile from home, she was attacked and soon afterwards murdered. The body was found at 1 o'clock, having three stabs in the neck and a severe cut on one hand. The body was about fifteen feet from the road and there was evidence that a great struggle had taken place in the road. A tramp had been in the neighborhood for a few days and several circumstances pointed very strongly to him as the one who perpetrated the deed.*

The Carroll County paper continued:

> *On Monday we learned that the party had been arrested and put in the Franklin jail. He was caught near Hogansville by the Sheriff of Heard County. The man's name is Waldrop and he formerly lived in this county and is well known to a great many of our citizens. He remained in Franklin*

Site of the Cragford Hanging Tree, 2013. *Photo by Beverly Crider.*

*jail until Monday evening when some 100 men or more from Alabama
came to Franklin and demanded him from the jailer. They said they did
not wish to destroy the jail, but that they had come after Waldrop and they
intended to have him. They finally by threats forced the jailer to give them
the key of the jail and they took Waldrop and carried him off. It was stated
by some of the party that they intended to take Waldrop back to the place
where the deed was committed.*

A correspondent of the *Atlanta Constitution* wrote that Hal Mitchell attended
the hanging of Waldrop, who saw him in the crowd. Pointing to Mitchell,
Waldrop said, "You are the man who got me into this scrape; you offered
me seventy-five dollars to kill your wife, and I made the mistake of killing Al
Mitchell's wife." Mitchell denied the charge, and Waldrop recounted to the
crowd the details of the transaction.

Waldrop was hanged in front of about six hundred witnesses on the site
where he murdered Mrs. Mitchell. In 1949, a memorial marker was placed
at this location in what is now Cragford.

In Memory of the tragic death of Mrs. Lobina Knight Mitchell June 30,
1881 by the cruel hands of Charles J. Waldrop age 24 who was hanged
on this spot by the public July 3, 1881
Erected by M.D. Amason
Commissioner District No. 3
Clay County Alabama 1949

CHAPTER 50

KRING COFFIN SHOP

The Kring Coffin Shop, erected circa 1860–70, was the showroom for coffins built by Edward Kring. Here you would pick out the material and wood for your coffin, which would then be custom built.

Kring was probably the busiest builder in Gainesville in the 1870s. Not only a builder of coffins, he also built both the Methodist and Episcopal churches, as well as several homes and businesses. He had a large workshop at the rear of the coffin shop and also a large barn or warehouse to store

Kring Coffin Shop in Gainesville, Alabama, 2013. *Photo by Beverly Crider.*

materials. Kring's coffin shop is included in the Gainesville Historic District that's listed on the National Register of Historic Places.

The coffin shop is located in Gainestown, Alabama, on the east side of Highway 39 approximately 0.2 miles south of the river bridge.

CHAPTER 51

STAR WOUND IN WETUMPKA

S tructurally disturbed." For decades, that's how the Alabama Geological Survey described the jagged landscape of Wetumpka. It wasn't until 1972 that geologist Tony Neathery realized that Wetumpka sits "right on the bull's eye of the greatest natural disaster in Alabama's history." According to the Wetumpka Impact Crater Commission, the hills just east of downtown are the remains of a meteor crater measuring five miles wide. The blast happened when dinosaurs still roamed the earth, about

Wetumpka Impact Crater historical marker, 2013. *Photo by Beverly Crider.*

eighty-five million years ago, and would have destroyed all life for a radius of about forty miles.

The team surveying the area published its findings in 1976, calling the feature an astrobleme, which literally means a "star wound." The findings were met with skepticism, as geologists generally did not believe that large meteors could hit the Earth. In 1998, a research team headed by Auburn University geology professor David T. King Jr. found that the crater core contained shocked quartz, which can only be formed by an enormous explosion such as that caused by a meteor impact.

In 2002, the site became an internationally recognized impact crater. Scientists believe that at the time of the impact, the area was covered by a shallow sea up to one hundred feet in depth. Wetumpka is now regarded as the best-preserved marine impact crater in the world. Energy released by the impact was about 175,000 times greater than the nuclear explosion in Hiroshima in 1945.

CHAPTER 52

GOLD MINING IN ALABAMA

There's gold in them thar hills!" You may have heard those words in old westerns or school textbooks, but you probably never associated them with Alabama. Before the famous gold rush out west, however, Alabama was the place to be. The area known as the Goldville District in Tallapoosa County was so popular with prospectors that legend has it the amount of mail at the local post office rivaled that of New York City. Several east Alabama counties produced fifty thousand ounces of gold prior to the California strike. Between 1838 and 1860, coins were minted at the U.S. Mint in Dahlonega, Georgia, from gold extracted in Alabama.

In fact, there's still an old gold rush town in Tallapoosa County called Goldville. Now it's a tiny community, but when gold was discovered in the early 1840s, Goldville became a boomtown overnight, becoming one of Alabama's largest towns. With close to five thousand residents, Goldville boasted seven saloons, two hotels, a number of theaters and dozens of merchants.

The town lasted less than a decade until miners left for California for that big gold strike. When word of the California gold strike reached miners in Goldville, it is said that they packed up and left so quickly, they didn't even bother putting out their campfires. Many of the old Alabama gold mines were submerged when Lake Martin was filled in 1926.

Gold mining and panning remains a popular hobby in the area, and there are several gold-bearing streams and branches in the Talladega National Forest and on private property. Other Alabama counties located in the

Monument erected in honor of the Alabama town of Goldville in Tallapoosa County, home of Alabama's gold rush, 2013. *Photo by Beverly Crider.*

Upper Gold Belt include Randolph, Talladega, Clay, Tallapoosa, Coosa, Chambers, Elmore, Shelby and Chilton.

Goldville remembers its legacy with a historical monument that reads:

> *GOLDVILLE*
>
> *Goldville, Alabama, incorporated on January 25, 1843, was at one time one of the largest cities in Alabama with a population of near 5,000 With the coming of the California gold rush in 1849 the city became a dormant municipality later to be reinstated on July 9, 1973*

CHAPTER 53

BIRMINGHAM'S UNDERGROUND RIVER

Marine monsters once dragged ships of a prehistoric race from what is now Birmingham to the Gulf of Mexico via an underground river. Not convinced? Would you believe that Birmingham was in danger of collapsing into that underground river and being swept away? Legends have been passed down through the years about this "Mystic River," as it was called.

Much of the Birmingham area lies on a bed of primarily limestone, which is a relatively soft, sedimentary rock, easily worn and shaped by eons of water flow. Add to that slightly acidic runoff, and you have the ingredients for the formation of caverns, which become sinkholes when they collapse. The area is certainly known for that. But what about an actual river underground?

A writer named Joe Mulhatton visited Birmingham in 1883, when he read an account of a small flowing stream discovered by a well driller in the city. He began expanding the story into a sensational report of a huge river flowing beneath the city, threatening the safety of the citizens above. His fictional report first appeared in the *Louisville Courier-Journal* and was later picked up by numerous papers. He claimed the city of Birmingham rested on a "crust" of stone only a few feet thick and that many buildings had collapsed after that crust had broken open during construction of a large building. He even claimed that city hall had settled four feet on one corner. The story spread like wildfire when it was printed. For two days, the telegraph office was overwhelmed with telegrams from all over the country asking if the story were true.

Underground Rivers, by Richard Heggen, cited the November 29, 1884 edition of the *Saturday Evening Post,* in which Professor Mulhatton stated:

> *The great subterranean stream recently discovered under the city of Birmingham is undoubtedly the most remarkable discovery ever made on the American continent. The river is greater in volume than the mighty Mississippi. Its vast subterranean bed is undoubtedly due to the grinding and cutting of immense icebergs during the glacial period. Then at a subsequent preadamite period violent upheavals of the earth toppled over the mountains which forms the present grand archway through which the iceberg continued to cut leaving it as it is now—a natural ship canal to the Gulf of Mexico. A prehistoric race undoubtedly utilized it for the transportation of metals from this section to the sea where they were transported to various points of the world. Furnaces on a scale scarcely so magnificent yet as satisfactory in results to those prehistoric people undoubtedly existed on the present site of Birmingham, as ruins of those, and of ancient sun-temples are found in various parts of the country.*
>
> *Added to this, we discovered in niches of the cave numerous articles of bronze, also statuary, numerous Masonic emblems, and mummies with sandals on their feet —all in perfect state of preservation. We also discovered the remains of marine monsters on the dais or old red sandstone period, prominent among them the huge Ichthyosaurus, which was undoubtedly used by these prehistoric races to drag their ships from what is now Birmingham to the Gulf of Mexico. These extinct sea monsters were docile and harmless, and were harnessed to the ships laden with pig iron, which they pulled to the sea with the greatest of ease. They were more powerful than the most powerful locomotives of the present day. Hulls of these subterranean ships are scattered all along the banks of this great subterranean stream.*

It was hard to suppress such a sensational story. An article in the March 25, 1886 edition of the *Atlanta Constitution* announced:

> *Much excitement exists over the report made today by W.C. Kerr, who is boring artesian wells for the water supply of the Birmingham rolling mills. Two holes have been bored a depth of five hundred feet beneath the surface. Water, pure and clear, filled the wells within twelve feet of the top. It was announced by Mr. Kerr that the water came from an underground stream, the size of a village creek, on which is built the city water works. The*

stream is large enough in places for boats. Persons placed their ears to the top of the hole, and heard the water rushing below.

Stories more in the realm of possibility were collected by Walter Bryant in a 1975 *Birmingham News* article:

- Native Americans informed early settlers of an underground stream that ran the full length of the county.
- R.H.L. Wharton purchased the "water privilege" for the infant city in 1871 and dug wells on Second Avenue North at Twentieth and between Twentieth and Twenty-first Streets. The latter well was reported to have struck an underground stream.
- An office in the vicinity of Fifth Avenue North and Twenty-second Street advertised "Mystic Underground River" excursions during the 1880s and 1890s.
- Access to an underground stream near Highland Avenue and 12 Avenue South was sealed by the city in the early 1900s because it posed a danger to children.
- Construction of the Tutwiler Hotel (1914) was delayed by the need to add steel beams to the foundation in order to span the river's cavern.
- The Florentine Building (1927), which was planned as a ten-story building, had only two stories, due in part to the expense of shoring the foundation.
- The Federal Reserve Building's 1957 annex was hit with foundation flooding. The excavation filled with clear water and was pumped out continuously during construction.
- Construction of the Daniel Building (1967) was delayed as engineers searched for areas of solid bedrock between limestone cavities.
- Numerous downtown structures are said to use underground water, reached by wells, as part of their cooling systems.

More recently, in January 2013, a sinkhole, reportedly more than one hundred feet deep, appeared near the intersection of Fifteenth Street and Third Avenue South during construction of Regions Field.

So the legend of the "Mystic River" continues. Is the river real? Does Birmingham have a lot of groundwater playing havoc with the city's architecture? Factor in one more piece of information as you ponder the question.

"It is a common misconception that groundwater is found in underground rivers like those that form limestone caverns," according to the Alabama State Water Program. "In fact, groundwater is more like the water in a sponge, held within the tiny pores of the surrounding aquifer material. It is important to note that the rate of groundwater flow, especially in confined systems, is very slow compared to the flow of water on the surface. It is typically in the range of several inches per year to several feet per year."

So what do you think of our mighty underground river system? Does it belong in books of science or legend?

CHAPTER 54

QUIRKY TOWN NAMES

Alabama, as any other state, has its share of downright silly names. Some names can be traced to their origins, while others have back stories that might or might not be accurate. Here are just some of the cities and towns located in Central Alabama, a mere fraction of the total number of strange Alabama place names.

The Bottle, a community in Lee County, was named for "the world's largest bottle," located in the area from 1924 to 1933. John F. Williams, the owner of the Nehi Bottling Company, constructed the sixty-four-foot-tall bottle-shaped building, nicknamed the "Nehi Inn." The Bottle contained a grocery store and service station on the ground floor, with living quarters and storage on the second and third floors. Before the Bottle burned down in 1933, President Franklin Delano Roosevelt visited following a trip to Auburn. Although the building hasn't been around for more than eighty years, the land it stood on is still listed as "The Bottle" on maps.

Bug Tussle near Smith Lake in Cullman County was allegedly named after an intoxicated local was found lying in the dirt, waiting for a stagecoach, watching a couple of beetles "tussle" in the dirt.

Cragford in Clay County was first called Wesobulga but was changed to Cragford in 1907 by the Atlanta, Birmingham & Atlantic Railroad. The town was across Crooked Creek from the depot. There was no bridge, so crossing the creek was accomplished by fording. Since the village was on a craggy hill, the town became known as Crag-ford or "Crag and Ford."

Eclectic in Elmore County was suggested by M.L. Fielder, who had taken an "eclectic" course of study in school. To him, the word meant "that which is best."

Frog Eye (or Frogeye), located in Tallapoosa County, was named during Prohibition. A saloon in the community sold both legal and illegal liquor. A ceramic frog sat in the saloon window to alert customers when the "state boys" were there. If they were, the owner would close one of the frog's eyes so customers would know not to ask for the illegal alcohol. If both the frog's eyes were open, it was safe to order the illegal stock. The community became known simply as Frog Eye.

Hell's Half Acre, now known simply as Half Acre, is located in Marengo County. The traditional explanation is that after completing their work, surveyors found they had made a half-acre error. They assigned the extra land to the devil, calling it "Hell's Half Acre."

Intercourse, located in Sumter County, was named for the crossroads where the general store sits. Story has it a sign was posted outside the town's meeting hall promoting the local ladies' sewing instruction group. It read, "Intercourse Lessons Wednesday Night." After several car crashes at that intersection, the good ladies were asked to remove the sign.

New Site is located in Tallapoosa County. Legend has it people moved here because they found the neighboring community of Goldville to be a sinful city.

Reform in Pickens County was supposedly named after sinful residents ran an evangelist out of town. As he left, he yelled, "Reform! Reform!" over his shoulder.

Remlap, located in Blount County, was named in 1882 by the town's first postmaster, James W. Palmer. He wanted to name the town for himself, but his brother Perry had already founded Palmer in Jefferson County. So, James gave his town their last name spelled backward.

Slapout in Elmore County is adjacent to Holtville. The owner of a country store would tell customers who asked for out-of-stock items, "I'm slap out." Folks just started calling the area Slapout.

Smuteye in Bullock County has one of the more entertaining back stories. The town blacksmith's shop became quite the gathering place for men to talk and drink. They would stand around the fire in the winter and drink moonshine. As the story goes, staying close to the fire left their faces covered with smut, covering everything but their eyes. When they got home, their wives would take one look at their smutty faces and know where they had been. The women began calling the blacksmith shop "Smuteye," and soon folks called the community "Smuteye."

CHAPTER 55

WORLD WAR II GERMAN POWS HELD IN RURAL ALABAMA

In 1942, at the conclusion of the campaign in North Africa, the logistical strain of securing such a large number of prisoners in the area prompted the U.S. military to move the POWs to the United States. The U.S. Army Corps of Engineers rapidly established camps in nearly every U.S. state to house them. Alabama's first camps were constructed during the winter of 1942–43. Army doctrine dictated that camps be built either at existing military bases or at sites distant from major cities and industrial centers. The army first selected two sites near the rural Alabama towns of Aliceville and Opelika, located in western Pickens County and eastern Lee County, respectively.

Aliceville's initial influx of prisoners (members of Rommel's elite AfrikaKorps, who had been captured and held in detention camps in North Africa until the prison was ready) started arriving by train in May 1943. Eventually, the camp held over six thousand prisoners, among the largest German POW camps in the United States. Almost all prisoners were German soldiers; however, some Italian POWs from the European theater joined them. The camp employed more than one thousand American military and civilian personnel.

Camp Aliceville was composed of four hundred frame buildings: barracks, a hospital, bakeries, chapels, a greenhouse, theaters, a water and sewer system, a fire department, an amphitheater, sports fields and gardens. It was a barbed-wire compound with guard towers.

Army engineers established another camp for three thousand prisoners at Fort McClellan, located in Calhoun County, and a fourth camp for two thousand prisoners was added in February 1944 at Fort Rucker in Dale County.

Camp Aliceville has become widely regarded as a model of humane treatment of POWs. The American military stocked abundant provisions for the dietary and recreational needs of the prisoners. Life within the camps was so comfortable that some Alabama residents resented what they perceived as the POWs' pampering while they endured rationing.

Daily life for prisoners consisted largely of work and leisure. During their free time, prisoners participated in a variety of activities, such as soccer, and some even formed orchestras. Each of the major camps established a newspaper that featured prisoner essays, articles, short fiction, puzzles and cartoons.

Each major camp also established a camp college, and prisoners could enroll in a wide variety of courses, including history, mathematics, the sciences, vocational courses and preparatory classes for students seeking postwar careers in medicine, law, electrical engineering and architecture.

Following Germany's surrender in the spring of 1945, Alabama's POWs were repatriated to their homelands. During the years of postwar reconstruction, a number of former POWs returned to Alabama. Little exists of their former sites of imprisonment, however. By 1947, the camps had been dismantled, and today there is little evidence that the camps ever existed.

Camp Aliceville is the main focus of the nearby Aliceville Museum, established in 1995. It has also been the subject of books (*Guests Behind the Barbed Wire*, by Ruth Beaumont Cook) and a History Channel documentary.

The museum houses what is said to be the largest collection of World War II POW memorabilia in the United States. It features permanent exhibits on Camp Aliceville; the Aliceville Coca-Cola Bottling Company, which was active from 1910 to 1978; and an extensive collection of U.S. military uniforms and equipment.

CHAPTER 56

COON DOG CEMETERY

A coon dog and his human are not easily parted. Death is probably the only way to accomplish this monumental feat. So it's not too surprising that one hunter felt the need to memorialize his longtime friend and hunting companion Troop by giving him a burial befitting a champion.

Troop died the day before Labor Day in 1937. Troop's hunting partner, Key Underwood, joined by several friends, buried Troop on September 4 where they all loved to camp and hunt: a pine bluff known as "Sugar Creek." Underwood marked Troop's grave with a large stone bearing Troop's name and his birth and death dates, which he engraved with a hammer and chisel. Although it wasn't his original intention, Key had just established the world's only Coon Dog Cemetery (according to a sign on the site).

Several years later, Underwood's brother buried one of his coon dogs at the same location, so the men decided they needed to protect the site. They leased the area from a lumber company that owned the land at that time and named the cemetery the Key Underwood Memorial Graveyard.

Located in a remote area of Colbert County known as Freedom Hills Wildlife Management Area near the Natchez Trace and the community of Cherokee, the cemetery is the final resting place for more than 150 coon dogs. It's quite an adventure finding the place, but that doesn't stop some seven thousand people from visiting each year.

The land now belongs to the Alabama Department of Conservation and Natural Resources, but the Tennessee Valley Coon Hunters Association oversees the cemetery. Many of the grave markers are hand chiseled by the

Monument in the Coon Dog Cemetery in Colbert County, 2012. *Photo by Beverly Crider.*

owners, but some have been professionally made. Listed among the dead are Patches, Preacher, Smoky and Night Ranger. And etched along with these names are tributes such as, "A joy to hunt with" and "He wasn't the best, but he was the best I ever had."

A granite monument of two dogs barking up a tree marks the entrance to the cemetery.

Until the digital age, word of mouth was the only way people found out about the Coon Dog Cemetery. Today, the Internet has helped spread the word of this unique Alabama attraction. The 2002 movie *Sweet Home Alabama* even included a scene featuring a re-created version of the graveyard. Several world champion coon dogs are at rest here, including Hunter's Famous Amos, Ralston Purina's Dog of the Year in 1984.

The cemetery is still open for interments, but the Coon Hunters Association must verify that the dog is an authentic coon dog. A pedigree is not required, but the dog must have been a hunting dog and must have hunted raccoons exclusively.

CHAPTER 57

THE OCTAGON HOUSE

Claudia Waddell Harris, a mystery writer in the early twentieth century, used the abandoned basement of Barbour County's Octagon House for the setting of one of her most successful short stories, "The Rusty Key." The story was sold to *Mystery Magazine* in New York City and is one of four short stories in her collection, *The Rusty Key: Prize Stories of the Deep South*. The house had a storied history before that, however.

Constructed between 1859 and 1861 by businessman Benjamin Franklin Petty, it is believed to be the only surviving antebellum home of purely octagonal design in the southeastern United States that made use of the "gravel wall" building method to create what is commonly referred to as a "concrete house."

During the Civil War, the house served as the headquarters of Union troops who occupied Clayton on April 28, 1865. Petty offered his home to Union brevet major general Benjamin H. Grierson in hope that it would not be looted or destroyed by the invading army.

The basement of the home, which would later provide such inspiration to author Claudia Harris, was excavated three feet below ground level to take advantage of natural cooling. It has five rooms and a combination stairwell-hall. The winter kitchen includes a large fireplace used for cooking and a small room for storage. The workroom, which was also used as a dining room, includes a large pantry and is the only full-sized room in the house with its own outside door. Both the kitchen and the workroom have brick floors. The stairwell-hall has a stone floor, includes an area for fuel storage

Octagon House in Clayton, Alabama, 2012. *Photo by Beverly Crider.*

and functions as the work entrance to the basement. A large dirt-floored cellar completes the basement plan.

The Octagon House passed to Petty's daughter and her husband in 1899, but the young couple did not need such a large house. At that time, Claudia and her husband, Judge Bob T. Roberts, offered a "trade plus cash" deal in which they swapped their home for the Octagon House and paid the couple the difference in the value of the two homes.

When the Robertses' daughter Mary married William C. Beaty in the mid-1920s, the second floor was made into a separate apartment for the couple. The Beatys inherited the house from the Robertses and drastically modified the structure, building a two-story addition at the back entrance that included kitchens and bathrooms. The one-story porch on the front was replaced by a much larger two-story porch. A new outside stairway was constructed, and windows on both the first and second floor were converted to entrance doors. The original entrance hall was used as an office, and the door was replaced by a window. The inside stairs between the first and second floors were removed, and the area became a closet.

William Beaty died in 1958, and in 1971, Mary married Elliot Armistead, a descendant of one of the founders of the city of Montgomery. After Mary's death in 1973, Armistead lived in the Octagon House until his death. During the later years of his life, he rented the second-floor apartment to Oats Caraway, a native of Clayton and a history enthusiast, who conducted the research necessary to earn the home a place on the National Register of Historic Places in 1974. It also is an Alabama Historical Landmark.

In 1981, the town of Clayton, through the efforts of then mayor Ed Ventress, purchased the Octagon House from the estate of Mary Roberts Beaty Armistead and set up the Clayton Historic Preservation Authority to facilitate its restoration and preservation. The commission oversaw efforts to restore, repaint and furnish the house to its original appearance, with gray walls and forest green trim. The structure was restored to its pre-1920s appearance and today has twelve large rooms, ten small rooms, ten closets, thirty-seven windows, four outside doors and thirty-one inside doors. The home now serves as an event facility operated by the Town of Clayton.

CHAPTER 58

HITLER'S TYPEWRITER IN THE BESSEMER HALL OF HISTORY

An Alabama Great Southern Railway depot (later Southern Railway) built in 1916 in Bessemer, Alabama, is home to an unlikely piece of world history: Hitler's typewriter.

The depot, placed on the National Register of Historic Places in 1973, houses the Bessemer Hall of History Museum and an extensive image archive, early newspapers, clothing and artifacts illustrating Bessemer's history as a mining, steelmaking and rail center.

Perhaps the most popular exhibit, however, is a German Groma 1930s typewriter, known as "Hitler's typewriter." It was discovered in storage in

Hitler's typewriter, on display at the Bessemer Hall of History Museum, 2012. *Photo by Beverly Crider.*

Bessemer Hall of History Museum in Bessemer, Alabama, 2012. The museum is housed in the former Alabama Great Southern Railway (later Southern Railway) depot built in 1916 in downtown Bessemer. The depot ended operation in the early 1970s. It sat unused for many years until it was rededicated as the Hall of History in the 1980s. *Photo by Beverly Crider.*

the museum's basement in the mid-1980s with notation that it had been captured by the Allies at Adolf Hitler's mountain hideaway, the Eagle's Nest, at the end of World War II. Visitors from around the globe have traveled to Bessemer to see it.

Among the many other fascinating exhibits in the museum, you will find an International Time Recording Machine or, as it's called today by so many of us hourly wage earners, a "time clock," manufactured by a company now known as IBM. Also featured is an impressive collection of antique telephones, military helmets, Native American artifacts, horse saddles and railroad memorabilia.

A Pullman Standard boxcar (commemorating the one millionth boxcar) located just across the street from the museum houses a remarkable railroad exhibit. A local club named the Wrecking Crew has filled the boxcar with a working model railroad display, depicting downtown Bessemer circa 1950 from the perspective of the spot currently occupied by the boxcar.

CHAPTER 59

BRIDGING THE BIGBEE WITH COCKS

In the early days of the automobile, cars were produced at a much quicker pace than the roads they traveled on. "Hitting the open road" could, quite literally, mean "hitting the road," in many cases. Having to contend with mud, boulders, streams and other adverse terrain meant an extremely slow trip and, likely, a damaged vehicle. And then there were the horses and assorted other animals that shared the road. The days before paved roads were not the best of times for motorists.

If you decided to venture outside territory you knew, there were no road signs to guide your way—at least nothing resembling the signs we're familiar with today. Roads had no official names, and motorists basically followed paths that were marked by paint on trees or arrows nailed to poles along the way.

As the number of cars increased, it became obvious that someone had to develop a better way for getting around in them. The Automobile Club of Savannah came up with the idea for the Dixie Overland Highway (DOH) in July 1914. It would be known as the "Shortest and Only Year Round Ocean to Ocean Highway." The DOH, which was one of the first "named" auto trails in America, connected Savannah, Georgia, on the Atlantic with San Diego, California, on the Pacific. It corresponds almost exactly with today's U.S. Highway 80, which travels through Alabama's Black Belt.

The March 1917 issue of *Better Roads and Streets* carried an association press release that summarized the history of the organization:

In July, 1914, the Automobile Club of Savannah, Georgia, made a path-finding tour across the State of Georgia to Columbus. They found a practical route, one-half of which was constructed road. A meeting was held in Columbus. It was determined to secure the construction of the entire highway...The object of the association being to promote the construction and use of a highway through the States of Georgia, Alabama, Mississippi, Louisiana, Texas, New Mexico, Arizona, and California.

The press release went on to say:

It was then developed that the Dixie Overland Highway when constructed will be the shortest, straightest, and only year round, ocean to ocean highway, in the United States. All highways east of the Mississippi and the most of those west of the river, are laid out for north and south travel. The Dixie Overland connects them all, is a trunk line through the heart of the "black belt," crossing the rivers at the head of navigation, and forming what the promoters believe to be the most useful and important highway in the South.

It is valuable for the transportation of passengers in business and pleasure cars. It will be used in the next step in the evolution of transportation for the exchange of light, and short distance freight. Its location and advantages will make it of particular value for military purposes.

After several years of work on the project, the association realized that the only major waterway east of the Mississippi River without an adequate bridge was the Tombigbee River in Demopolis. Once built, that bridge would be "one of the most important single connecting links of the entire distance."

While excited at the prospect of having such an important structure in their city, Demopolis residents, as well as their counterparts on the west side of the river, had no way to fund the building of such a bridge. It was time to call in a professional fundraiser. Frank Derby of Sumter County had successfully raised funds for the American Red Cross, as well as helped with the funding of a smaller bridge in York, Alabama. When he was asked to head up the DOH project in Demopolis, he jumped at the chance.

Derby developed a campaign amusingly called "Bridge the Bigbee with Cocks." The plan was to auction roosters donated not only by area residents but "famous people" as well. He believed the good-natured competition would encourage more generous bids. The contract between Derby and the DOH committee stipulated that Derby would receive a payment of $25,000 only if the rooster auction netted $75,000.

Derby began soliciting roosters from politicians and celebrities while word of the magnificent rooster auction spread across the country. It even gained the support of both the secretary of the navy and the secretary of war. While at a peace conference in Versailles after World War I, Admiral William Benson and Secretary of the Navy Josephus Daniels informed President Woodrow Wilson, as well as the leaders of England, France and Italy, of the upcoming festivities. Each agreed to send a gamecock to Demopolis and to pay the entry fee.

President Wilson presented the elite roosters to the Demopolis and Alabama delegation in a ceremony on the White House steps. The August 10, 1919 edition of the *New York Times* featured the ceremony on the front page. International coverage soon followed, including in the *London Times*. The famous birds traveled from Washington to Alabama by train and even spent a night in the bridal suite at the Tutwiler Hotel in Birmingham, according to a 2003 article in *Alabama Heritage*. Roosters arrived from all over the country, including birds from comedian Fatty Arbuckle, Mary Pickford and Alabama's own Helen Keller, who dyed a small hen blue and called her "Little Blue Hen."

Roosters being presented to Alabama citizens at the White House.

After all was said and done, President Wilson's rooster received the highest bid at the auction: $55,000. When proceeds were tallied, the pledges totaled between $200,000 and $300,000. The excitement of the festivities had apparently gotten the better of many attendees as the amount actually paid to the DOH association totaled just $65,000. Even payment for the president's rooster never arrived. After a deduction of $20,000 for expenses, only $45,000 remained to apply toward construction of the bridge.

Due to lack of funds, construction was delayed until 1922, when the state agreed to move forward, adding federal funds to the rooster auction proceeds. On May 15, 1925, Memorial Bridge opened. To the people of Demopolis, however, it was always known as "Rooster Bridge." In 1959, the Alabama state legislature voted to officially change the name to "Rooster Bridge" in honor of Derby's auction.

The original bridge eventually became outdated and had to be replaced in 1980. But, thanks to a 1971 resolution passed by the Alabama legislature, any bridge or bridges that cross the Tombigbee River at that point shall bear the name "Rooster Bridge."

Rooster Bridge in Demopolis.

The Dixie Overland Highway has been largely forgotten over the years, but Alabama's section of U.S. 80 still carries the name. One month before final approval was given for the establishment of the U.S. Numbered Highway System in November 1926, DOH association president Ed Fletcher took a Cadillac sedan across the highway from San Diego to Savannah in a single-car timed race. He and his team completed the 2,535-mile run in seventy-one hours and fifteen minutes. At that time, only about 5 percent of the highway had hard surface.

CHAPTER 60

TOMBSTONES WITH A STORY TO TELL

THE "LADY STATUE" AT OLD MEMPHIS CEMETERY

There's a monument in Old Memphis Cemetery near Aliceville known as the "Lady Statue." It's a mourning stone, sometimes known as a weeper (not to be confused with the "Weeping Angels" on *Doctor Who*). You won't turn to stone if you get too near. According to the book *Alabama Cemeteries*, legend has it that James A. Coleman Jr. (1855–1884) married his young bride only a few years before he met with an untimely death. Grief-stricken, she commissioned a monument from Italy to be carved in her likeness so she could watch over her beloved for eternity. Actually, stones depicting mourners were not uncommon during that time, so who is to say if this one actually bears her likeness.

The monument was originally installed to face eastward, as is the tradition for headstones. In this position, the statue's arms extended across the grave of her husband, who was considered to be a distinguished citizen in the town of Memphis, Alabama. Sometime later, according to the most popular account of the tale, Mrs. Coleman learned that her husband had been unfaithful to her. After overcoming her initial shock, the outraged young widow had the monument turned to face the opposite direction, thereby "turning her back" on her cheating husband.

According to another account, after the monument finally arrived from Italy, the family thought it was too beautiful to face the river. They

The "Lady Statue" at Old Memphis Cemetery near Aliceville, Alabama, 2013. *Photo by Beverly Crider.*

decided to face it west so that people traveling along the nearby road could also admire its beauty.

George Washington's Bodyguard

Just down the road from the "Lady Statue" in Old Bethany Cemetery in Pickens County is a memorial to James McCrory, bodyguard to George Washington at Valley Forge, Pennsylvania. McCrory's wife, Jane, is buried alongside him. A native of Ireland, McCrory quickly became a strong supporter of his new land and enlisted in the Continental army shortly after arriving in America.

In addition to serving as bodyguard of General Washington, McCrory also took part in at least five battles after serving at Valley Forge during the winter of 1777–78. After the war, he and his family helped establish the town of Vienna, Alabama.

The epitaph on McCrory's tombstone reads: "In Memory of James McCrory. Died Nov. 24th, 1840, aged 82 years, 6 months and 9 days. The deceased was a soldier of the Revolution and was at the battles of Germantown, Brandywine and Guilford Courthouse, and was one of Washington's life guards at Valley Forge and served his country faithfully during the war. Peace be to the soldier's dust."

Little Nadine's Playhouse

A beautifully maintained dollhouse sits in the Oakwood Cemetery in Lanett, Alabama, as a decades-old memorial to little Nadine Earles. The four-year-old came down with diphtheria and died just a week before Christmas in 1933. Her big request for Christmas was a dollhouse, so her father decided to make her wish come true. He began constructing the playhouse in the family's backyard, but the family was placed under quarantine due to Nadine's illness, and he had to stop.

Nadine died before her gift could be completed. City officials allowed her father to build the dollhouse around her grave as a loving tribute to his daughter. The child's toys and other belongings were placed inside. Nadine's dollhouse is now among the country's popular memorials. Residents of Lanett still care for the house. The Town and Country Garden Club places seasonal decorations on the house and switches out dolls every Christmas.

Little Nadine's Playhouse in Oakwood Cemetery in Lanett, Alabama, 2013. *Photo by Beverly Crider.*

THE CASTELLI OBELISK

At the turn of the twentieth century, the Italian population in West Blocton, Alabama, was not welcome in the general community. Many Italians were laborers in the area mines, and those who were brought to this country by mine bosses worked in an enclosure known as a "dog pen" until they paid off the cost of their passage.

Segregation was so strong that white residents refused to allow an Italian child to be buried at the traditional white cemetery, Mount Carmel. This prompted the bishop of the Catholic Diocese of Alabama to consecrate an Italian cemetery in 1901.

For many years, the cemetery remained in an area of West Blocton that was hard to reach due to the treacherous condition of the road leading up the ridge. Many grave markers are etched in Italian, and some feature small oval portraits of the deceased. The hard lives and deaths of the immigrants are reflected in many of the inscriptions.

Perhaps the most famous of the markers is an obelisk for a woman who was butchered with a hatchet at her family's store in the "Little Italy" section of West Blocton.

"Here lie the ashes of poor deceased Elizabetha Castelli," the Italian inscription reads, "born in 1864 murdered at the young age of 36 years, robbed and killed by a murderer of the black race in the morning at 8 o'clock on December 15, 1902, leaving behind her husband and son, weeping and sobbing."

According to a 2007 article in the *Tuscaloosa News*, a suspect, Ed Walker, was arrested with a large sum of money on him. He was tried in Centreville the following April. Walker claimed it was a white man named Bud Red who actually committed the murder of Mrs. Castelli. The jury convicted Walker in less than an hour and sentenced him to death by hanging.

As this was only the second time there had been an official execution on the gallows in Bibb County since 1865, it created quite a bit of excitement. After the hanging, the rope was cut into pieces and handed out to witnesses as souvenirs.

WITCH OF CRAGFORD

Mary Sunday (circa 1780–1865) is buried in the Cragford Wesobulga Cemetery in Clay County. However, her body was not laid to rest according to standard Christian burial practices, which gave rise to rumors about her character.

Burial site of Mary Sunday, the "Witch of Cragford," in the Cragford Wesobulga Cemetery in Clay County, 2013. *Photo by Beverly Crider.*

A traditional Christian burial positions the coffin facing east, so the deceased is able to witness the Second Coming of Jesus. Mary was buried in a north–south position. According to some old traditions, this would indicate she had committed suicide or had been labeled a witch.

Of course, at the time that Mary was buried, the method for determining true east was very unreliable. Even though the magnetic compass existed at the time of the country's first settlers, it was rarely used. It was more common to determine east based on the position of the sun at sunrise, which changed every day of the year.

Whatever the reason for her burial position, Mary has become known among some locals as the "Cragford Witch."

BIBLIOGRAPHY

BOOKS

Bell, Landon Covington. *The Old Free State: A Contribution to the History of Lunenburg County and Southside Virginia.* N.p.: Genealogical Publishing, 1974.

Bogdan, Robert. *Freak Show: Presenting Human Oddities for Amusement and Profit.* Chicago: University of Chicago Press, 1990.

Booth, Donna J. *Alabama Cemeteries.* Birmingham, AL: Crane Hill Publishing, 1999.

Duncan, Andy. *Alabama Curiosities.* 2nd ed. Guilford, CT: Globe Pequot Press, 2009.

Foscue, Virginia O. *Place Names in Alabama.* Tuscaloosa: University of Alabama Press, 1989.

Guiley, Rosemary. *Monsters of West Virginia: Mysterious Creatures in the Mountain State.* Mechanicsburg, PA: Stackpole Books, 2012.

Kazek, Kelly. *Christmas Tales of Alabama.* Charleston, SC: The History Press, 2011.

McClelland, Stewart Winning. *A Monument to the Memory of John Wilkes Booth.* Indianapolis: University of Indiana, 1951.

Miller, Elaine Hobson. *Myths, Mysteries, & Legends of Alabama.* Birmingham, AL: Seacoast Publishing, 1995.

Smith, Michelle. *Legends, Lore and True Tales of the Chattahoochee.* Charleston, SC: The History Press, 2013.

Walsh, William S. *Handy-Book of Literary Curiosities*. Philadelphia: J.B. Lippincott Company, 1892.

Windham, Kathryn Tucker. *Alabama: One Big Front Porch*. Montgomery, AL: New South Books, 2007.

Magazines and Newspaper Articles

Baggett, James L. "Louise Wooster, Birmingham's Magdalen." *Alabama Heritage*, issue 78 (Fall 2005).

Crownover, Danny. "John Pratt, Early Typewriter Inventor from This Area." *(Gadsden, AL) Messenger*, September 14, 2012.

Gardner, Earle. "Bodyguard of George Washington Buried in Cemetery in Pickens." *Tuscaloosa News*, February 17, 1963.

Garst, John. "Chasing John Henry in Alabama and Mississippi: A Personal Memoir of Work in Progress Tributaries." *Journal of the Alabama Folklife Association*, no. 5 (2002): 92–129.

Goodson, Mike. "Strange Sights Spotted Along Coosa River." *Gadsden Times*, September 27, 2009.

Key, William. "Sky Devil-Ship Scares Pilots; Air Chief Wishes He Had One." *Atlanta Journal*, July 25, 1948.

Mellown, Robert O. "Dixon Hall Lewis: An Alabama Silhouette." *Alabama Heritage*, no. 47 (Winter 1998).

Milwakee Journal, July 10, 1982.

Payne, Ricky. "Popeye Grew Up on the Coosa River." *Rome News-Tribune*, February 11, 1979.

Ress, Thomas V. "James McCrory: Alabama's Revolutionary War Hero." *Alabama Heritage*, no. 103 (Winter 2012).

Reynolds, Ed. "Runaway Bridegroom." *Black & White*, June 30, 2005.

Riley, Patsy. "Visiting Mrs. Teel." *Alabama Heritage*, no. 94 (Fall 2009).

(Salt Lake City) Desert News. "The Hueytown Hum Creates a Clamor." April 16, 1992.

Smothers, Ronald. "Hueytown Journal: Humming Along, and Howling Mad." *New York Times*, April 14, 1992.

Tuscaloosa News. "Nation's Largest Sinkhole May Be Near Montevallo." March 29, 1973.

Wade, Elizabeth W. "Remembering Mrs. Rena." *Alabama Heritage*, no. 94 (Fall 2009).

Wall, Randy. "Inside the Wire: Aliceville and the AfrikaKorps." *Alabama Heritage*, no. 7 (Winter 1988).

Welborn, Aaron. "A Seer in Selma." *Alabama Heritage*, no. 67 (Winter 2003).

Whisenhunt, Dan. "Anniston's James Bond." *Anniston Star*, August 10, 2008.

Willis, Becky. "Rooster Bridge." *Alabama Heritage*, no. 67 (Winter 2003).

Windham, Ben. "Southern Lights: Robert Van de Graaff Never Recieved His Due in Tuscaloosa." *Tuscaloosa News*, December 12, 2004.

WEBSITES AND BLOGS

Acker, Amber. "Community of Rockford's Adoration for Former Town Dog to Be the Focus of New Documentary." January 16, 2013. http://www.al.com/living/index.ssf/2013/01/community_of_rockfords_love_fo.html.

Alabama Confidential. "December Giant aka Golly Hole Montevallo, Alabama 1972." May 17, 2010. http://alabamacorruption.blogspot.com/2010/05/december-giant-aka-golly-hole.html.

Alabama Journal (Associated Press). "First Windshield Wiper Found No Place in Market." February 14, 1972. http://bplonline.cdmhost.com/cdm/singleitem/collection/p4017coll6/id/122/rec/1.

Alabama Outdoors magazine. "The Alabama Bigfoot Society." March 26, 2012. http://www.aothemagazine.com/?p=333.

Alabama State Water Program. "Are There Rivers Underground?" http://www.aces.edu/waterquality/faq/faq_results.php3?rowid=1687.

Al.com. "Strange Alabama." http://blog.al.com/strange-alabama/index.html.

Allen, Frank. "The Truth About Black Panthers and Bears in Alabama." Outdoor Alabama. http://outdooralabama.com/hunting/hunterresources/articles/truth.cfm.

American Physical Society. "This Month in Physics History, February 12, 1935: Patent Granted for Van de Graaff Generator." http://www.aps.org/publications/apsnews/201102/physicshistory.cfm.

American Roads. "Dixie Overland Highway." http://www.americanroads.us/autotrails/dixieoverland.html.

Ayers, Linda S. "History of Wesobulga/Cragford." Roots Web. http://archiver.rootsweb.ancestry.com/th/read/DEAN/2010-09/1285821165.

Bessemer Hall of History. http://www.bessemerhallofhistory.org/.

BhamWiki. "Humphry Osmond." http://www.bhamwiki.com/w/Humphry_Osmond.

———. "Loulie Jean Norman." http://www.bhamwiki.com/wiki/index. php?title=Loulie_Jean_Normanxcdz.

———. "Storyteller Fountain." http://www.bhamwiki.com/w/Storyteller_ fountain.

———. "Timothy Leary." http://www.bhamwiki.com/w/Timothy_Leary.

———. "Underground River." http://www.bhamwiki.com/w/Underground_river.

———. "Virginia Hill." http://www.bhamwiki.com/w/Virginia_Hill.

———. "Willie Perry." http://www.bhamwiki.com/w/Batman.

Bigfoot Encounters. http://www.bigfootencounters.com/.

Birmingham History Center, 1807 Blog Avenue. "Oo-OOOH-oo-oo-oo-oo-oo-ooohh…" August 1, 2011. http://birminghamhistorycenter. wordpress.com/2011/08/01/oo-oooh-oo-oo-oo-oo-oo-ooohh/.

Buchanan, Mary Jo. "Talladega Speedway Tries to Tame the Demons That 'Haunt' the Track." Bleacher Report, October 31, 2009. http:// bleacherreport.com/articles/282105-talladega-speedway-tries-to-tame-the-demons-that-haunt-the-track.

Bullock, Randy. "Dr. Lewis Archer Boswell: Inventor of the Arial Boat." Alabama Aviator. http://www.alabamaaviator.com/isaa.asp?id=72868.

Calvert, Scott. "Fred, the Town Dog: R.I.P." *Baltimore Sun*, January 17, 2003. http://articles.baltimoresun.com/2003-01-17/news/0301170255_1_ fred-town-dog-rockford.

Carruth, Barbara Woolbright. "Rube Burrow." http://fayette.net/Carruth/ rubeburrowmain.htm.

Conger, Cristen. "Top 10 Famous Female Sideshow Freaks." http:// entertainment.howstuffworks.com/arts/circus-arts/10-female-sideshow-freaks.htm.

Cruz, Gilbert. "Miracle Cross Garden; Prattville, AL." *Time* magazine, July 28, 2010. http://content.time.com/time/specials/packages/ article/0,28804,2006404_2006095_2006138,00.html #ixzz2nLMJCtL9.

Cuthbert, Matt. "Oak Mountain Tunnel, Leeds, Alabama: Haunted by John Henry?" http://blog.al.com/goforth/2007/04/oak_mountain_tunnel_ leeds_alab.htmlhttp://www.npr.org/programs/morning/features/patc/ johnhenry/.

Denney, Jim. "Lost Gold Mines." Lake Magazine. http://lake. lakemartinmagazine.com/2012/04/11/lost-gold-mines/.

DeSoto Caverns Park. http://desotocavernspark.com.

Dogwood Books and Antiques. Roman Chronicles vol. 1, no. 2: "Popeye and the Coosa River." http://www.mullinsmania.com/romanchronicles/ v1n2.htm.

Dubosky, John. http://pabook.libraries.psu.edu/palitmap/bios/Leary__
Timothy.html.

Edwards, Bob. "Dixon Hall Lewis." Find a Grave. http://www.findagrave.
com/cgi-bin/fg.cgi?page=gr&GRid=3277.

Ellington, M.J. "A Star Fell on Sylacauga." *Decatur Daily* Online Edition,
November 30, 2006. http://archive.decaturdaily.com/decaturdaily/
news/061130/meteorite.shtml.

Ensey, Tom. "Paranormal Investigation: Bear Creek Swamp Near Prattville's
Definitely Creepy, But Is It Haunted?" October 19, 2010. http://prattville.
wsfa.com/content/paranormal-investigation-bear-creek-swamp-near-
prattvilles-definitely-creepy-it-haunted.

Examiner.com. "Little Remains of Historic Gold Mining Town." http://
www.examiner.com/article/little-remains-of-historic-gold-mining-town.

Explore Southern History. "Pink Parker's Unusual Tribute." http://www.
exploresouthernhistory.com/boothmonument.html.

Fernandes, Andrea. "27 Buildings Shaped Like Food That's Sold There."
Mental Floss. http://mentalfloss.com/article/29909/27-buildings-
shaped-food-thats-sold-there#ixzz2pDNSZiDg.

Findagrave.com. "Virginia Hill." http://www.findagrave.com/cgi-bin/
fg.cgi?page=gr&GRid=11213.

———. "William Yeldell Cosper." http://www.findagrave.com/cgi-bin/
fg.cgi?page=gr&GRid=114887333.

Fleming, Frank. "Joe Louis." http://www.history.com/topics/joe-louis.

Forbes, Dennis. "Tracking Innovation: Windshield Wipers." *InventorsEye: The
USPTO's Bimonthly Publication for the Independent Inventor Community.* http://www.
uspto.gov/inventors/independent/eye/201302/Windshield_Wipers.jsp.

Franklin, Wayne. "Meet Rube Burrow, King of the Outlaws." June 22, 2011.
RealSouthernMen.com.

Gamel, Dortha. "James McCrory—George Washington's Bodyguard."
GenForum. http://genforum.genealogy.com/mccrory/messages/651.html.

Garner, George. "Gold Production in Alabama." Encyclopedia of Alabama.
http://www.encyclopediaofalabama.org/face/Article.jsp?id=h-1666.

Geological Survey of Alabama. "Sinkholes in Alabama." http://gsa.state.
al.us/gsa/geologichazards/Sinkholes_AL.htm.

Gribben, Mark. "The Myth of Mob Gallantry." TruTv. http://www.trutv.
com/library/crime/gangsters_outlaws/mob_bosses/women/3.html.

Hall, John C. "Hodges Meteorite Strike (Sylacauga Aerolite)." Encyclopedia
of Alabama. http://www.encyclopediaofalabama.org/face/Article.
jsp?id=h-1280.

Harris, Mike. "Talladega Jinx Gets Halloween Test." October 27, 2009. http://www.racintoday.com/archives/11422.

Heggen, Richard. *Underground Rivers*. Google eBook. August 11, 2013.

Hinton, Ed. "They're Hearing Voices at Talladega." ESPN.com, April 3, 2009. http://m.espn.go.com/rpm/story?storyId=4090615&src=desktop.

Historic Resources of Gainesville. "The Coffin Shope." http://pdfhost. focus.nps.gov/docs/NRHP/Text/85002930.pdf.

IMDB.com. "Loulie Jean Norman." http://www.imdb.com/name/nm0635560/bio?ref_=nm_ov_bio_sm#trivia.

Jimmerson, Ellin Sterne. "Louise Wooster." Encyclopedia of Alabama. http://www.encyclopediaofalabama.org/face/Article.jsp?id=h-1862.

Katz, Elanine. "Hazel Farris." http://www.bhamwiki.com/w/Hazel_Farris.

Kazek, Kelly. "Car-sized Catfish? Supernatural Serpents? 'Monster Fish' Host Zeb Hogan Discusses Alabama's Legendary River Creatures." June 26, 2013. http://www.al.com/living/index.ssf/2013/06/car-sized_catfish_supernatural.html.

———. "5 Mythical Creatures That Reportedly Roam Alabama's Back Roads." October 16, 2013. http://www.al.com/living/index.ssf/2013/10/5_mythical_creatures_that_repo.html.

Kidd, Jessica Fordham. "Herman Blount (Sun Ra)." Encyclopedia of Alabama. http://www.encyclopediaofalabama.org/face/Article.jsp?id=h-1896.

King, David T., Jr. "Wetumpka Crater." Encyclopedia of Alabama. http://www.encyclopediaofalabama.org/face/Article.jsp?id=h-1035.

Lewis, Herbert J. "Jim." "Joe Louis." Encyclopedia of Alabama. http://www.encyclopediaofalabama.org/face/Article.jsp?id=h-1601.

Library of Congress. "Local Legacies, DeSoto Caverns." http://lcweb2.loc.gov/diglib/legacies/AL/200002662.html.

———. "Local Legacies, Roanoke, Alabama: Home of the Ella Smith Doll." http://lcweb2.loc.gov/diglib/legacies/AL/200002658.html.

Linneweber, Colin. "Statue Erected in Alabama for Joe Louis, Boxing Great and Adolf Hitler Enemy." Bleacher Report, February 23, 2010. http://bleacherreport.com/articles/351207-statue-erected-in-alabama-for-boxing-great-hitler-enemy.

Loulie Jean Norman Memorial Site. http://louliejeannorman.memory-of.com/.

"Mary Anderson: Windshield Wipers." Inventor of the Week Archive, September 2001. http://web.mit.edu/invent/iow/anderson.html.

McFall, Anna. "Abbey's Historic Ave Maria Grotto Untouched by Tornado." *Gadsden Times* (Associated Press), May 13, 2011. http://www.gadsdentimes.com/article/20110513/WIRE/110519865?p=1&tc=pg#gsc.tab=0.

McKeown, Blanche. "She Invented the Windshield Wiper." January 1956. Birmingham Public Library. http://bplonline.cdmhost.com/cdm/compoundobject/collection/p4017coll6/id/1265.

Murphy, Frank. "Ra, Sun (Herman Poole Blount)." Encyclopedia of Jazz Musicians. http://www.jazz.com/encyclopedia/ra-sun-herman.

National Geographic Channel. *Mummy Roadshow.* "An Unwanted Mummy," episode 12, April 1, 2002. http://www.youtube.com/watch?v=6jAQeHCghK0.

Nobel, Justin. "The True Story of History's Only Known Meteorite Victim." *National Geographic Daily News,* February 20, 2013. http://news.nationalgeographic.com/news/2013/02/130220-russia-meteorite-ann-hodges-science-space-hit/.

"Old West Outlaws." LegendsofAmerica.com.

Olive, J. Fred, III. "Mary Anderson." Encyclopedia of Alabama, University of Alabama at Birmingham. http://www.encyclopediaofalabama.org/face/Article.jsp?id=h-2553.

Pednaud, J. Tithonus. "Myrtle Corbin: The Four-Legged Woman." http://thehumanmarvels.com/118/myrtle-corbin-the-four-legged-woman/parasitic-twins.

Project 1947. "The Chiles-Whitted 'Rocketship' Sighting." http://www.project1947.com/gr/chileswhitted.htm.

Ragsdale, Barbara. "Sacred Heart of Jesus Catholic Church, Cullman, To Host a Year-Long Centennial Celebration." *Cullman Times.* http://www.cullmantimes.com/religion/x1296870330/Sacred-Heart-of-Jesus-Catholic-Church-Cullman-to-host-a-year-long-centennial-celebration.

Rainer, David. "Panthers in Alabama: Fact or Folklore." Outdoor Alabama. http://www.outdooralabama.com/oaonline/panthers08.cfm.

Raines, Ben. "Florida Is the Sinkhole King, but Alabama Is Not Far Behind." March 5, 2013. http://blog.al.com/wire/2013/03/florida_is_the_sinkhole_king_b.html.

Roadside America. "Cross Garden: Hell's Warning Label." http://www.roadsideamerica.com/story/2019.

———. "Grave of Edgar Cayce, Famous Prophet." http://www.roadsideamerica.com/story/12606.

———. "Hitler's Tea Service and Spy Weapons." http://www.roadsideamerica.com/story/10065.

———. "Ram-Headed Southern Storyteller." http://www.roadsideamerica.com/story/17168.

Robinson, John. "Josephine Myrtle Corbin." http://www.sideshowworld.com/76-Blow/Myrtle/Corbin-1.html.

Rootsweb. "More About the Four-Legged Woman of Blount County." April 23, 2009. http://listsearches.rootsweb.com/th/read/ALBLOUNT/2009-04/1240495231.

———. "More About Waldrop." *Carroll County Times*, July 15, 1881. http://archiver.rootsweb.ancestry.com/th/read/DEAN/2010-09/1285821165.

———. "Outrageous Crime." *Carroll County Times*, July 8, 1881. http://archiver.rootsweb.ancestry.com/th/read/DEAN/2010-09/1285821165.

Rural Southwest Alabama. "The Coffin Shop at Gainesville." http://www.ruralswalabama.org/attractions/the-coffin-shop-at-gainesville-al/.

Sacred Harp Musical Association. "Sacred Harp Singing." http://fasola.org/.

Sacred Heart Catholic Church. http://www.sacredheartchurchcullman.org/history.htm.

Schwartz, Larry. "'Brown Bomber' Was a Hero to All." http://espn.go.com/sportscentury/features/00016109.html.

The Skeptic's Dictionary. "Edgar Cayce." http://www.skepdic.com/cayce.html.

Skunkapes.com: The Official SkunkApe Tracking Website. http://www.skunkapes.com/index.htm.

Sutton, Amber. "SyFy Channel Series to Shine Light on Prattville's Paranormal Activity During Tonight's Episode." http://www.al.com/entertainment/index.ssf/2013/04/syfy_channel_series_to_shine_l.html.

Swallow a Bicycle Theatre. "Josephene 'Myrtle' Corbin, the Four-Legged Girl." http://www.swallowabicycle.com/performances/freak-show-2013/josephene-myrtle-corbin-the-four-legged-girl/.

Telegraph (UK). "Dr. Humphrey Osmond." February 16, 2004. http://www.telegraph.co.uk/news/obituaries/1454436/Dr-Humphrey-Osmond.html.

Tennessee GenWeb. "Sickness and Death in the Old South." http://www.tngenweb.org/darkside/facing-east.html.

Thomas, John D. "Arms and the Man: Alumnus Farley Berman Owns One of the World's Most Extensive Private Collections of Historic Weaponry." *Emory Magazine*, Winter 1997. https://www.emory.edu/EMORY_MAGAZINE/winter97/fberman.html.

Time magazine. "Crime: Murder in Beverly Hills." June 30, 1947. http://content.time.com/time/magazine/article/0,9171,854710,00.html#ixzz2oXl71GTQ.

Treggiden, Katie. "The History of Typewriters." Confessions of a Design Geek. http://confessionsofadesigngeek.com/2013/07/17/feature-the-history-of-typewriters/.

UFO Casebook. "The Chiles/Whitted Sighting." http://ufocasebook.com/Chiles.html.

Ulrich, Jennifer. "Transmissions from the Timothy Leary Papers: The Self-Annotated Papers." New York Public Library. http://www.nypl.org/blog/2012/04/17/transmissions-timothy-leary-self-annotated-papers.

United States House of Representatives: History, Art and Archives. "The Life of Representative Dixon Hall Lewis of Alabama." http://history.house.gov/HistoricalHighlight/Detail/36746.

Vess, Thomas V. "DeSoto Caverns." Encyclopedia of Alabama. http://www.encyclopediaofalabama.org/face/Article.jsp?id=h-3243.

Visit West Alabama. "Aliceville Museum." http://www.visitwestalabama.com/mediaportal/aliceville_muse/index.html?videoID=16.

Ward, Rufus. "Ask Rufus: Rube Burrows: 'King of the Outlaws,' the Most Feared Train Robber." August 15, 2010. http://www.cdispatch.com/lifestyles/article.asp?aid=7380&TRID=1&TID=.

Waters, Joe. "Gold Mining History Tallapoosa County, Alabama." http://jovikri.tripod.com/public-index.html.

Weingroff, Richard F. "U.S. Route 80: The Dixie Overland Highway." U.S. Department of Transportation Federal Highway Administration. http://www.fhwa.dot.gov/infrastructure/us80.cfm.

Wetumpka Impact Crater Commission. http://www.wetumpkaimpactcratercommission.com/Default.asp?ID=597&pg=FAQS.

Williams, John M. "The Legend of Rena Teel." *Like the Dew: A Journal of Southern Culture and Politics*, May 26, 2011. http://likethedew.com/2011/05/26/the-legend-of-rena-teel/.

Wilson, Claire M. "Rube Burrow." Encyclopedia of Alabama. http://www.encyclopediaofalabama.org/face/Article.jsp?id=h-2950.

Windham, Ben. "Southern Lights: South Seethed with Hatred." *Tuscaloosa News*, April 26, 2012. http://www.tuscaloosanews.com/article/20120826/NEWS/120829840?p=1&tc=pg#gsc.tab=0.

———. "West Blocton Cemeteries Rich in Local History." *Tuscaloosa News*, January 14, 2007. http://www.tuscaloosanews.com/article/20070114/NEWS/701140364?p=4&tc=pg.

WTVM (Columbus, GA). "Lanett Cemetery Dollhouse Is Memorial to Little Girl." http://www.wtvm.com/story/7138239/lanett-cemetery-dollhouse-is-memorial-to-little-girl.

Yanow, Scott. "About Sun Ra." http://www.mtv.com/artists/sun-ra/biography/.

ABOUT THE AUTHOR

Beverly Crider is a freelance writer with a background in media relations and web design. Back in pre-Internet days, she founded the Magic City BBS, a dial-up computer bulletin board system that introduced Alabama to its first online newspaper, the *Birmingham Post-Herald*.

An Alabama native and proud graduate of the University of Alabama, Beverly and her husband, Kyle, currently travel the back roads and forgotten haunts of the state in search of material for her blog, "Strange Alabama," on AL.com and on Facebook. When it's time to put pen to paper (or pixel to screen), she's usually surrounded by her five furry children, also known as the "Crider Critters," who provide their own form of inspiration. For more information about Alabama's history, folklore and fun places to travel, visit StrangeAlabama.com.

Visit us at
www.historypress.net
....
This title is also available as an e-book